Shine on Harvey Moon

VOLUME 2
OF HARVEY MOON'S MEMOIRS

As told to
Laurence Marks, Maurice Gran and Micheál Jacob

 B⊞XTREE WitzEnd.

First published in Britain in 1995 by Boxtree Limited, Broadwall House,
21 Broadwall, London SE1 9PL

Picture credits:
© Central Independent Television plc: pages 20; 21; 30; 43; 45; 47;
48; 51; 54; 70; 73
Hulton Deutsch Picture Library: pages 6; 10; 14; 17; 18; 19; 42; 79;
118; 121
Matthew May: page 11
All other photographs © Meridan Broadcasting Limited

Designed by Dan Newman

Printed in Great Britain by Bath Press Colourbooks, Glasgow

ISBN: 0-7522-0663-X

A CIP catalogue record for this book is available from the British Library

CONTENTS

LORD GEORGE BROWN

BROTHERS (AND, NATURALLY, SISTERS)! I am honoured to have been asked to write these few words of introduction to the Memoirs of my old friend and loyal colleague Harvey Moon. A staunch Labourite, fellow Londoner and man of similar height to myself, Harvey was one of those unsung foot soldiers of the Socialist brigade until I plucked him from obscurity to serve as my Parliamentary Under Secretary at the Department of Economic Affairs. I cannot now quite remember why, but I can clearly recall, with the aid of my scrapbooks, the excitements through which he and I lived as comrades and friends.

It was in October 1964 that Labour swept to power under Harold Wilson's leadership. Although he and I had our differences, and although many said my own leadership would have been preferable, we set personal considerations aside jointly to lead Britain into a new era of peace, prosperity and planning. Harold paid me the compliment of creating a new ministry and placing me at its head. The Department of Economic Affairs burned like a beacon at the heart of government. Out went the old-style Tory approach of stop-go economics; in came a new-style Labour approach of economics a go-go, so in tune with the times.

I myself was responsible for a Declaration of Intent, signed by both sides of industry and designed to introduce the first genuine policy on incomes to which all could subscribe. The fact that many thousands of workers were granted increases rather higher than the guidelines illustrates not the failure of the policy, but rather the international conspiracy, headed by the Gnomes of Zurich, which set out to undermine our efforts.

Nothing daunted, we pressed on with a great National Plan, which envisaged a growth in the economy of 25 per cent over five years. Although the country was actually producing fewer goods at the time, the pound was nose-diving and we had a majority

Opposite: *Lord George Brown at the Department of Economic Affairs*

of two, we still believed that nothing could stand in our way. To my surprise, after two glorious years, the Department was abolished and I moved on first to become Foreign Secretary, then to lose my seat, while Harvey returned to the obscurity of the back benches. Such is politics!

In his flattering letter inviting me to supply these few words, Harvey recalls that he regularly supported me as we tried to find my car and driver after long nights of planning, fired only by our shared enthusiasm for change and frequent recourse to the juice of the barley. I confess that my own recollections are rather more vague.

However, I am pleased that the wit and wisdom of my old colleague should reach a wider audience, thanks to the good offices of another comrade, Captain Maxwell. I commend this book wholeheartedly – it will occupy a unique place among the memoirs of former Hackney councillors.

THE MOON MEMOIRS

℘℮

I T WAS WITH A CERTAIN DEGREE OF ANXIETY that I yielded to the urgent
pleadings of my publishers and agreed to set pen to paper. Although my career
has been long and distinguished, even, I suggest in all humility, unique, a certain
modesty has governed my life. Who, I wondered, would wish to read the scattered
reminiscences of an old war-horse, now virtually out to grass, albeit not having run
to seed? Several agreeable lunches, visits to hospitality boxes at sporting events, a
very thoughtful case of vintage Moët, and the unlimited services of a skilled visiting
masseuse, helped to persuade me that I may still have something to say as Britain
approaches the Millennium, standing on the dawn of a new era, poised on the precipice
of the unknown.

Footballer, Justice of the Peace, Councillor, Member of Parliament, life peer, friend
of the famous and keeper of the Socialist conscience, I can truly say that my life has
not been free of incident. Even now, my door is always open to the younger generation
who carry the heat and burden of the day, provided of course that they make a prior
appointment! Naturally, I jest, and although modesty forbids me to name those who
have sought my advice, I wish here to thank Tony and Cherie, John, Gordon, Robin,
Margaret and Dr Jack for their many kindnesses.

Modesty was not the only consideration which kept me from the not inconsiderable
task of trawling through the memories of a lifetime. There was also an unhappy
experience to take into account, since I suffered in the past, as did so many, at the
hands of the late Member for Buckingham North, perhaps now better known as the
late Robert Maxwell.

As a longstanding and significant figure in the party to which I have devoted my
life, I made a special point of befriending new Members, showing them around the
House, explaining the rather complicated proceedings, and introducing them to the
wider world of London where temptations lurk for the unwary.

Maxwell was one such, and at first he appeared almost pathetically grateful to be taken under the wing of a figure such as myself, who had achieved the gratifyingly dizzy heights of Parliamentary Under Secretary in the Department of Economic Affairs under my old friend and quaffing partner George Brown. Allowing 'Bob', as he insisted I call him, to involve me in various of his schemes seemed a small return for the hospitality which he seemed always eager to lavish upon me. We were, at the time, inseparable, an example of the fraternal spirit in which I have invariably conducted my political dealings. A somewhat distasteful graffito in one of the Commons lavatories, portraying me with my tongue in a Maxwellian orifice, was the product of a diseased mind, and a complete misunderstanding of our relationship.

Although the results of investments in some of Maxwell's business ventures often turned out to be disappointing, I could not help but be flattered when he suggested that I should compile a volume of Memoirs. Saying that he knew my political and personal anecdotes by heart, adding flatteringly that he could recite them in his sleep, he told me that one of his several publishing companies would be honoured to publish the book. It would only cost me £1,000, a not inconsiderable sum of money in those days but, he assured me, well worth it, as was the cost of publicity, a further £1,000. Naively, I said I understood that such matters did not work in the way he explained – surely publishers generally paid their authors? Maxwell explained that this was indeed the case, but in this instance no publisher could do justice to the manuscript without

Robert Maxwell, MP for Buckingham North

subsidy. The volume would be produced to the highest possible standards (here he went into some technical jargon which I confess I could not follow), and was destined to be such a bestseller that I would recover my modest initial outlay.

Thus encouraged, I set to work with a will, seamlessly weaving my political exploits into a kaleidoscopic tapestry of family reminiscence. Maxwell told me that readers wanted to know the whole man, and the whole man was what I gave them, omitting only those events which would perhaps give readers a false impression of my honour and probity, since the ambiguities and complexities of life can frequently mislead those not in the know.

Having finished the manuscript, and solicited a foreword from my old boss and mentor, George Brown, I committed it to Maxwell's care. I was regularly reassured over the succeeding months that I should soon hold the volume in my hands, and would then be able to bask in the acclaim that would surely follow. The Nobel Prize for Literature was mentioned. Imagine my distress when I found on my doorstep two ill-wrapped brown paper parcels, plastered with Romanian stamps, and a demand from the Post Office to pay several pounds in excess. Far from being the fine volume that had been promised, the book was printed on what appeared to be old-fashioned lavatory paper, the shiny sort which older readers will recall with a shudder. The type demanded a magnifying glass, the text was littered with misspellings, a section of what appeared to be a Chinese textbook was interpolated, and as I picked a book at random it fell apart in my hands. The author's name appeared as Arvie Mon.

Naturally I made determined attempts to contact Maxwell, but he was apparently on an extended visit to Eastern Europe, and his underlings were unable to advise me as to when he would return. Making the best of a bad job, I despatched copies to the major libraries, journalists and political luminaries, not forgetting that bible of my youth, *Charles Buchan's Football Monthly*, retaining some half dozen for myself. Due to an unfortunate misunderstanding with a cleaning lady, five of these copies were used for lighting a fire, so only one copy remains in my possession. I have drawn on it to refresh my memory where necessary, and revised it where the passage of time has allowed greater frankness. Now, I fear, it has entirely disintegrated.

One of the few remaining copies of Volume 1 of my memoirs

However, since repetition is wearisome, I refer readers throughout this current volume, called for the purposes of logic and accuracy Volume 2, to Volume 1, which may be found in any of the great libraries. Anything of importance to students of my career is included here.

I should like to thank the research assistants with which my publishers have kindly supplied me. Laurence Marks, Maurice Gran and Micheál Jacob have laboured long and hard at my dictation, and have drawn on the works of other chroniclers of my life, from institutions as widespread as the University of California at Los Angeles, and the Hackney Working Men's Institute – Dick Clement and Ian La Frenais, Alan Clews, David Harsent, Gary Lawson and John Phelps, Francis Megahy, and Geoff Rowley.

In the words of my Baronial motto – *Velut inter ignis luna minores*.[1] Now let the truth be told!

---

1. Since Latin is now not widely known, I should explain that this is a quotation from the marvellous *Odes* of Horace, hitherto unknown to me but kindly drawn to my attention by the College of Heralds as we held protracted meetings over my coat of arms. It means: 'As shines the Moon among the lesser stars.' The coat of arms shows Diana the Huntress, symbolizing the moon, leaping lithely over a football boot, symbolizing my first career, aiming her bow towards a mug inscribed with the name Harvius, symbolizing my years of service to Burslem, with on the left hand side a golden letter 'H', again symbolizing my name. I am proud to wear this intriguing design on my blazer pocket, and have had it made up into tee-shirts over the years for the younger members of the Moon dynasty.

CHAPTER ONE

THE PEOPLE SPEAK

'CALL ME HARVEY!' That's what I said to the Queen at my first Buckingham Palace garden party, as I gave her a firm handshake and winked at the Duke of Edinburgh, but she moved on with a gracious smile. After that, although I have made no secret of my desire to trim the wealth and pomp of the Windsors, I was privileged to share many happy royal occasions and, although Her Majesty has always addressed me formally, I am told that, behind the scenes, the Duke invariably refers to me as "that cheeky bugger Moon". Recognition indeed!

I may be Baron Moon of Stoke Newington, I may live in a Georgian rectory in the delightful Hertfordshire countryside with six bedrooms and two acres of land, I may have a cook and gardener who live in, but make no mistake – I'm the same Harvey Moon who grew up barefoot in the East End. My dad, Charlie, was a brickie on twenty five shillings a week. My mum, Violet, was a ladies' maid before she got married. I played football down Mare Street with an old tin can, nicked apples off the market stalls, mitched off school to go swimming in the canal. Now I'm a Lord, writing this on a warm summer's day looking out over the garden, the birds are singing, and I've rung for my faithful Bridget to bring me a fresh pot of Earl Grey with some of those little biscuits from Fortnum's that I particularly like. It sounds like a nob's way of living, even a nabob's way of living! But I'm just plain Harvey, a simple man with simple tastes, although if people prefer to call me Lord Moon and it makes them feel more relaxed, then naturally I have no objection.

Opposite: *Moon the statesman strikes a Lordly pose*

My dear old mum and dad

As I have always argued, Socialism is about raising people up, not levelling down. Come the Socialist millennium, everyone will be able to choose how to live and the world will be a happier, fairer place where the birds will sing, the sun will shine, and Orient will be in the Premier Division. Please allow an old man his dreams.

It was a very different world when Hitler threatened to grind the people of Europe under the Nazi jackboot. As a lad, I was more interested in football than in the news. I would hear other people talking about what was going on, but my ambition was always to play for Arsenal and then for England. Left wing was my position, a prophetic place to play in view of later developments in my life! Of course, Mr Chamberlain and his piece of paper will always live in the memory, as the newsreel pictures live in the memories of everyone of my generation, but my main interest in life was Clapton (now Leyton) Orient, scoring goals, attempting to break into the first team, and hoping that a scout from Arsenal was watching. [2]

When war broke out I was among the first to volunteer. My hand–eye co-ordination, high level of fitness and quick brain, honed in the Orient reserves, led me straight to the RAF, where I confidently expected to become a pilot. However, the War Ministry in its wisdom felt that I would be better employed working as a stores clerk and so, after some basic training and some enjoyable games of football, I set sail on a troopship to Poona in India. Two friends I made there will feature later in these reminiscences.

---

2. For a full account of my early days, see *The Moon Memoirs*, Volume 1: *My Early Days*, Ceaucescu Press.

Suffice it now to say that, after my father's early death, Poona saw the second great tragedy of my life, and one that was to have a lasting impact on my post-war career.

The date was 23 March 1944. The sun was shining, but then it usually did. Temperatures out there threatened to send the mercury crashing out of the barometer more often than not. I remember saying to the Sergeant, "Looks like a hot one." "Yes, it does, Corporal," he replied.

Our base was outside the town, and we were a tight little band of pilots, mechanics and back-up staff, the boys in blue. I think it is true to say that without a well-organized stores operation the war could not have been won, and I can claim with all due modesty that the quality of filing in Poona was second to none.

However, all work and no play makes Jack a dull boy, and I must confess that, with my background in professional football, I was something of a celebrity in the base, serving not only as vice-captain of the football team, but also as unofficial trainer and tactician. In quieter moments I would practise dribbling around the shelving, heading against the filing cabinets, and playing keepy-uppy under the awning outside the stores hut. Of course, an officer was nominally in charge of the team, because that is the misguided way of the Services, and the manifest injustice of a Squadron Leader with two left feet captaining the side gave me an early insight into the injustice of the class system in general. But the lads knew where the real power lay and treated me accordingly.

In the days leading up to 23 March we had been doing intensive training for a match against the Gurkhas. These fierce fighting men, wiry little beggars who could creep up on you in the night and slit your throat without thinking twice about it, were not very skilful footballers, but they were determined. They coped better with the heat than we did, and when it came to tackling they took no prisoners!

The match was to be played in the early evening, when there was a bit of shade. The Gurkhas hadn't turned up as we gathered in the changing hut, but they arrived with their supporters in a couple of lorries, already wearing their strip.

In quieter moments I would practise dribbling around the shelving

The Squadron Leader – Jimmy Bond was his name – told us to keep our heads, keep our tempers, use our height advantage and wait for our superior skills to take effect. We had a bit of friendly rivalry over our respective scoring records; Bond was a few ahead of me. As we ran out to cheers, whistles and boos, he asked if I would be interested in a bet as to who would score the most during the game. I told him confidently I expected a hat-trick, and I can't say I liked the way he laughed.

The ref, one of our blokes, blew the whistle, and away we went. In the first ten minutes or so we didn't see much of the ball. Little fellows have a low centre of gravity, and those Gurkhas had certainly been putting some effort into their training since the last time we played. Somehow, the ball seemed to be glued to their boots. We tackled as hard as we could, and managed to keep them out. Then our centre-half, Nobby Adams, started to make an impression, and I began to see more of the ball.

Even now I think the most exciting thing in the world is to receive a perfect pass played just ahead of you, to dribble on, beat one man, beat another, have the centre forward screaming for the ball and decide whether to give it to him or to run in towards goal yourself, watching the keeper's eyes, trying to hypnotize him into moving the wrong way, leaving you more space to shoot at.

That's what happened on the evening of 23 March 1944. I got the ball. I beat one man. I beat another. I heard Bond calling for me to "Pass it, pass it, Corporal," and I thought – not on your nelly, officer.

I ran towards the goal, the goalkeeper ran towards me. I'm not a tall man, but I was looking down on him and I thought I'd chip the ball over his head into the net. I drew my foot back, but before I could make that sweet connection, their full back clattered into me from behind, and their keeper clattered into me from the front. There was a sort of scrunching noise I sometimes still hear in nightmares, and then an excruciating pain in my knee.

As it turned out, I scored, because the ball went under the keeper and into the net, although I was told later that Bond had kicked it when it was over the line and claimed

They say that grown men don't cry, but I'm not ashamed to admit that I cried. I bawled. I screamed. I writhed

it for himself. At the time, though, all I could think of was the pain. They say that grown men don't cry, but I'm not ashamed to admit that I cried. I bawled. I screamed. I writhed. I could see faces bending over me. Nobby asked me if I could walk. I told him, with only the minimum of profanity, that I couldn't.

Three of the lads helped me hop from the field and took me to the MO, but he prodded around, said he couldn't do much, gave me a jab and sent me off in an ambulance to Bombay General Hospital. There a very pleasant surgeon, Mr Singh, operated on my knee, removed the cartilage, and ended my career in football.

As I was lying in bed, recovering, Mr Singh used to pop by for a chat and to see how the knee was coming on. I told him my tales of the Orient, and he told me his. Although I spoke with my usual modesty, Mr Singh somehow got the impression that I was a celebrity, and he told me he would keep my cartilage in a glass jar among the hospital's memorabilia. For all I know, it is there to this day.[3]

Of course, the blow was devastating, and I persuaded myself that I could return to full fitness. But with the war news getting better, and our lads rolling back the Hun (with a little help from the Yanks), my thoughts turned to good old Blighty, and to my family. Although my old mum used to write, and I would hear occasionally from my daughter Maggie and Stanley, the nipper, there was never a line from my wife Rita, though mum said she was busy doing her bit to cement relations with the Allies.

I got back to England in November 1945 on a troopship. The dear old Thames was a sight for sore eyes, and when we docked at Tilbury I couldn't wait to get back to Hackney and take refuge in the bosom of my family. I jumped on to a bus that seemed to take for ever to reach the stop I so wanted to see. Finally it arrived and, wrapped up in my greatcoat against the unaccustomed cold, my kit bag over my shoulder, I made for the house and the warm welcome I was sure I would receive.

Although I had been told about it in letters and had seen pictures of it, there was

Opposite: the bombed-out remnants of my home

---

3. A detailed account of these events may be found in 'Footballing Days in the RAF' by Harvey Moon MP, Burslem News & Advertiser, 7 February 1955.

After the war everything was on ration

still something horrific about the bombed streets and derelict houses. It was a vision of hell, and I felt guilty that I had gone through the war in the comfort of Poona while my beloved East End had felt the full force of the Luftwaffe. That walk sowed the seeds of a determination to do something, to make England once again a land fit for heroes, a determination that would guide my footsteps into the hotbed of politics and provide me with the strength to climb the greasy pole of power.

Imagine my despair as I turned the corner, made my way towards the house, and found that there was no house there! My wife, my family, gone! Only the khazi was undamaged. I sank down on the seat, my head in my hands. Would malign fate always conspire against me? I heard someone whistling. It was the most cruel sound in the world. Then, like some kind of apparition, a postman appeared in the doorway and asked if I'd been caught short. My wife, I said, my kids. Gone! Yes, said the postman, up Tottenham way. Silly cow left the gas on and *boom!* He went off again, still whistling, but this time it sounded like Sir Malcolm Sargent conducting the Hallelujah Chorus with the massed ranks of the Huddersfield Choral Society. So I went home to my mum and the familiar flat in Ladysmith Dwellings.

Make no mistake, post-war life was difficult. Now it seems like another age, something from history books. I can see my great-grandchildren's eyes glaze over when I tell them about what it was like then. They can't feel it, they can't imagine it, perhaps they don't even believe me and think it's just the ramblings of an old man. Let me try to paint a picture for you.[4]

In India, we had enjoyed three square meals a day. We had clothes to wear. The sun shone. At home there was a strange kind of smell, a staleness in the air, a bit like boiled greens. There were bombed-out buildings and rubble, broken windows with wood nailed across the frames. And, the biggest shock of all, there was rationing. Everything was in short supply; the only thing there wasn't a shortage of was shortages. There were coupons for this, and coupons for that. You needed so many points for cigarettes, so many points for sweets. Soon after I got back, even bread was on the ration.

Opposite: *Denis Healey and Roy Jenkins in uniform at the Blackpool Conference of 1945, which I sadly missed*

Things changed a bit, of course, but basically what you got was 13 ounces of meat, $1\frac{1}{2}$ ounces of cheese, 6 ounces of butter or margarine, 8 ounces of sugar, 2 pints of milk, and 1 egg, per person, per week. It takes a bit of thinking about now, when an average lunch is smoked salmon with a rocket salad, followed by venison stew and two veg, with a nice bit of Stilton and perhaps some apple tart and cream to follow. Not to mention dinner.

---

4. For a lengthier version of my reminiscences on this period, see Chapter 3 of *The Moon Memoirs*, Volume 1, op. cit.

Even though I was more interested in football than politics, you couldn't avoid what the blokes were saying in the NAAFI during the war, and it was quite clear that change was in the air. Before the war it was the bosses giving the orders, and the workers doing what they were told. The Tories spread their black propaganda about Labour not being fit to govern. Then the war came, and suddenly the people who weren't fit to govern were in the government. And doing a bloody good job too (pardon my French). They were as patriotic as the next man, they were good ministers, and when the war was over they found themselves in charge of a party with the wind in its sails and the bit between its teeth. It was a young party, a dynamic party, a party determined to create a land fit for the heroes who had fought and won in the Army, the Navy and, of course, my own dear old RAF.

One of my great regrets over a long and, if I am allowed to say so, distinguished political career was that I did not attend the great Blackpool Conference of 1945 which set out its five-year programme of jobs for all, houses for all, and peace for all. Dashing young *Rita, my lovely* Major Denis Healey brought the conference to its feet when he called the upper classes *Margaret and* in every country "depraved, dissolute and decadent". Denis and I often laughed about *Stanley the nipper* that in later years as we swapped yarns in the tea-room at the Lords. Barbara Castle

danced with my old hero Herbert Morrison, as, later, she danced with me.[5] The electricity was such that, even in retrospect and even though I was not there, my old Socialist heart beats faster.

Young Stan was a handful for his mother and me

The other great talking point during the war was the need for a Welfare State, for Britain to become a country where the unemployed would be paid social security, where there would be free medical care, free education, and houses for those who needed them at reasonable rents. These were the great dreams which the Tories fought so hard to kill, and which the Labour Party fought to introduce. We in the forces had put our lives on the line in the cause of a better world, and a fairer society. We came home fired with a desire to turn our dreams into reality.

So that was the background facing me, then a humble RAF Corporal, as I picked up the threads of my life, renewed acquaintance with my family, and finally left the service with a demob suit of serviceable brown worsted, a pair of brogues, a titfer, and a cigarette ration that was worth its weight in gold. Great political change was in the wind, but the wind had not yet blown through Ladysmith Dwellings. I was not then thinking about the ship of state, but concentrating only on paddling the Moon canoe. Life was hard. I even took a job as Santa Claus at Burgess's department store, an

5. I repeat again my denial that Lady Castle and I were the "canoodling comrades and champagne-bibbing gossip-fodder" referred to in that scurrilous article 'Power – the Aphrodisiac', published in the 1960s by a Tory propaganda front organization and so-called national newspaper. 'Babs' and I were and are just good friends, as the late Lord Goodman made plain at the time.

experience I would not care to repeat. When little children become over-excited, one quickly discovers that red robes leave something to be desired in the waterproofing department.

My skills as a clerk seemed not to be in great demand, so I finally found employment operating a fly-press at Hartley and Son, a local company that made radio components. Mr Hartley (he was the son, apparently; there was no sign of any other Mr Hartley) ran the place like a sweat-shop, using antiquated equipment and paying starvation wages. He promised me that after a short while on the press I would be elevated to junior management status, but this – like so many of his promises – was entirely empty. As far as he was concerned, I was just another coolie. Although I was obviously better qualified than my workmates, I mucked in with the best of them, and soon assumed a leadership role. As a former Orient player, and with my wartime experience, they naturally looked to me and I, naturally, did my best for them.

My first skirmish with Hartley came on the day that I had to visit a possible school for my son, Stanley. Hartley grudgingly gave me time off, but his air of superiority got right up my nose. When I returned, I found there had been an accident. One of the girls had been injured when her arm was caught in one of Hartley's old machines, which naturally lacked any kind of safety guard. Hartley called for the first-aid kit, and told everyone to get back to work. I hit the roof. I demanded that Hartley got proper medical attention for my injured comrade, and said I would refuse to work until the union had approved the safety of every machine in the place. I appealed to

Lou 'One Lung' Lewis and my dear Maggie

my colleagues to join me. Much to my surprise, words sprang into my mind. Sentences came fully-formed. The muse of oratory had brushed me with her wings. I was given an ovation, and everyone downed tools until the union rep, Reg Merrick, arrived. Hartley fumed, but he could not sack us all.

Reg soon got things sorted to our satisfaction, if not to Hartley's, and he graciously complimented me on my political and organizational abilities. Why, he wanted to know, was I not a member of the Labour Party? I told him I was not a joiner, and for the moment he left it at that.

My next confrontation came shortly afterwards, bearing out the old adage that it never rains but it pours. My mum came to the factory to tell me that my daughter Margaret had unwittingly taken a job as a hostess in a house of ill-repute and that, even as we spoke, she was in danger of falling victim to the White Slave Trade (something about which the newspapers were full of stories at the time). With visions of my little girl being forcibly drugged with hashish and abducted to some Arabian seraglio, I tore off my overalls, grabbed my coat, and told Hartley it was an emergency. Hartley told me not to bother coming back. There was no time to argue; I just ran for a bus.

As was so often the case, my old RAF comrade Lou Lewis was the cause of the problem. Having taken a shine to Maggie, he was thrilled when his boss offered her a job, on the basis that all she would have to do was sit in a bar and encourage men to buy drinks. Since his boss was Conny Rosenthal – a spiv, gangster and all-round bad-hat, Lou might well have been suspicious, but he and Margaret were virtual babes in the wood at the time, and both were pleased at this new opportunity.

In this bleak period of my life, I was fortunate to meet a woman I will call Harriet, since this was her name

When I arrived at Rosenthal's drinking club, an insalubrious establishment in a seedy street on the fringes of the West End, I was shocked to find my former wife Rita behind the bar. Surely even Rita could not have stooped so low as to involve our daughter in the twilight world of hostesses and tired businessmen? She told me that the situation was entirely in hand, that she had resolved the matter to everyone's satisfaction, and that Margaret was free to leave. Rosenthal had invited Rita to become manageress of the club, and she had been pleased to accept.

Margaret, God bless her, was still entirely innocent of the peril she had so recently faced, sitting innocently in a booth waiting for me to take her home. I am not too proud to admit that I shed a fatherly tear as I held my little girl in a bear-hug and sobbed that I would always protect her. "Get off, dad," she said.

I went home to mum's flat and a bleak future. Sacked by a leering capitalist, chucked on the scrap-heap by a slave-driver, I was now unemployed. As I contemplated the dark horizon over a strong cup of tea, there came a knock on the door. It was a messenger from Hartley. All my comrades, those brave brothers and sisters, had downed tools and called an indefinite strike until I was reinstated! No Harvey, no work, was the message. Naturally I negotiated a bit of an improvement in my terms and conditions as a price for coming back, but Hartley was over a barrel, and he knew it. There were cheers when I walked into the factory, cheers that touched my heart as I was greeted with a rousing chorus of 'For he's a jolly good fellow'.

I suppose I should now come clean about my domestic arrangements at the time. Why, you may be asking, was I not living in Rita's Tottenham prefab, restored to the bosom of my family? Why was I living with my mum? The answer is simple – Rita refused to have me there. She had lived her own life through the war, and wanted to continue living it. As an early advocate of women's rights and freedoms, I naturally respected her decision, even though I found it hard to accept. I suggested to her, rationally but with all the force at my command, that she was a wastrel, an unfit mother, and that she should immediately mend her ways and welcome me back into her life. Using extremely unladylike language, she rejected my suggestions. Indeed, she threatened me with physical violence, so I beat a dignified retreat.

In my hour of need I found (as so often in my life) a comforter. From time to time during my career I have been accused of being a womaniser, to my mind a demonstrably false accusation. If I have an attraction to the opposite sex, it has always defeated me what it is. Ladies have told me many complimentary things which I blush to repeat, but words like handsome, charming, funny, unusual, dynamic and powerful have featured in my life, and I recall with pleasure memories which still have the power to make an old man happy.

I would have worked day and night to see my old mum well again

In this bleak period of my life, I was fortunate to meet a woman I will call Harriet, since this was her name. Our first encounter was on a formal matter; she was the headmistress of my son Stanley's school, and she was concerned that he was playing truant rather too often. She obviously took a keen interest in Stanley's welfare, and we struck up an immediate rapport. As we grew to know one another better, it transpired that she was secretary of Kensington South Labour Party, and also had an intimate knowledge of party affairs in Hackney, where the school was situated. Events at Hartley's had reached her ears, and she added her voice to that of Reg Merrick in encouraging me to become a party member.

Harriet was a perfect illustration of the broad church that is Socialism. Widowed when her husband, a test pilot, had crashed his aeroplane, she lived at the time with her aunt, a formidable woman who took an instant dislike to me. Harriet, though middle class, was truly a woman of the people. Her aunt was an inveterate snob, who tried hard to humiliate me, and set out to poison Harriet's mind against me. Harriet, God bless her, paid little attention, and it is to her that I owe the beginnings of my education in the finer things in life. She introduced me, for example, to the delights of vintage burgundy, for which I retain a lifelong enthusiasm. She loaned me books, and made me feel that even opera was not beyond the grasp of a straightforward working man.

Under her benign influence, I applied to become a member of the party to which I have devoted my life and such small talents as I may possess. At my vetting meeting she was there to lend moral support, and as Brother Merrick welcomed me into the fold I was certain that tears of pride were in her eyes.

She was, I suppose one would say now, a liberated woman. At the time I was a rather old-fashioned man, filled with romantic notions and the values that had been

Opposite: *Lou took this snap of me and my old Mum. If I look a bit funny, see page 29*

drilled into me by my mum and dad. To me, a lady was a lady, or – to put it more crudely – there should be nothing below the waist without an engagement ring. Harriet was impatient with these notions and, in true Socialist style and in a genuinely sisterly way, she told me to stop mucking about and get into bed, an invitation which politeness forced me to accept.

Then came a crisis. My mother became ill and delirious. In her agony, she made me promise that she would be allowed to die in her own bed. The doctor came, and diagnosed bronchial pneumonia, "the poor man's friend" as it was known in those prehistoric days. He held out little hope for her, unless I could afford to pay for penicillin injections. Would I let my mother die for the sake of a few pounds that I could ill afford but would nevertheless find? Of course not! Despite the iniquitous system, soon to be swept away in the glorious dawn of a truly national health service, putting the dustman and the duke on an equal footing, I would have worked day and night to see my old mum well again. The doctor was agreeable to weekly payments and, since he happened to have a sample in his bag, he gave the first injection at a reduced rate. The treatment, thank God, was successful, and my mother went to stay with her nephew in Northampton to recuperate and breathe some fresh country air.

I am an honest man, a straightforward man, a man who speaks his mind. It is a prescription I have used in my public life, as well as in my private affairs

Meanwhile, I was now in regular attendance at party meetings and at those fervent discussions, so valuable in the formulation of policy, which took place in the Trades and Labour Club bar. It was in the bar that I heard of the sad death of Councillor Coleman, who had represented Down's Ward with great distinction for many years.

Having absorbed the news, I made my way to the regular weekly meeting and, at the formal announcement of his death, I found myself on my feet making a speech which contained all the emotion evoked by my mother's illness. I spoke of the iniquities of the current system, of the outrageous cost of drugs, of how Councillor Coleman might have lived, of how my mother had been saved, but at a cost … again, I discovered the power of oratory, and found that I could make even the strongest weep. I urged that we should send a message to the government supporting the introduction of a National Health Service and, when a comrade pointed out that the service was already promised and being planned, I explained that I was in the process of arguing that the message should call for its introduction as speedily as possible.

I was stunned and surprised when, after this speech, I was approached by Brother Merrick and asked if I would consider standing for Down's Ward as Dave Coleman's successor. Naturally I pointed out my inexperience, but it appeared to be no barrier and soon, to my amazement, I was fighting my first election campaign.

My mother, now returned from Northampton, was a tower of strength. Her first reaction to the news was that it was not for "the likes of us" to be running things but, even though she did not share my political opinions, she placed a high value on family loyalty, and her standing in the neighbourhood helped immensely as we went knocking on doors and soliciting votes. I found an immense fund of goodwill among the good people of Hackney, whom I had the honour to serve for eight years until I fell victim to a left-wing plot, a scurrilous episode in the history of the local party that I will describe later in these reminiscences. At the time I was neither left nor right, just an honest man striving to do his best for the people, and conscious of the unexpected honour which had been bestowed on him.

My opponent, a Tory fighting under the banner of the Progressive Party (a misnomer if ever there was one), was a Major Saxby. Our first encounter was at Hartley's, where he came to solicit votes. Always a fair person, I offered him my hand, letting him feel the honest sweat and grease that is the daily lot of the working man. Rather ostentatiously, I thought, he wiped his hand on a rag, and closeted himself with Hartley. Through the glass window I could see them deep in conversation, with many glances at me. I assumed, rightly as it transpired, that they wished me ill.

Saxby and I, with the other candidates, were invited to take part in a public meeting chaired by the Vicar of St John's. One of the hard lessons of my life is that appearances count for as much in politics as does sincerity, a rather disgraceful state of affairs to my mind. I am an honest man, a straightforward man, a man who speaks his mind. It is a prescription I have used in my public life, as well as in my private affairs.

However, appearances demanded that I should appear on the platform as a family man, so I went to see Rita. She was at first unwilling to offer her support, but when I pointed out that, as a Councillor, I might be able to have something done about structural deficiencies in her prefab, she agreed to join me at the meeting.

Flanked by her and my mother, I listened as politely as I could to Saxby's patronizing address, then rose to my feet, greeted by warm applause and, I am sure I recall, cries of "Good old Harvey!". I spoke to the crowd as man to man, and I felt them responding as I outlined my vision of a Socialist Utopia, bringing Jerusalem again to Hackney's green and pleasant land and marshes. Naturally there was an ovation. Then the Vicar called for questions. A man in the audience said he had a question for Saxby. Would he like to say a few words about the value of family life?

Saxby made great play with the fact that he was an officer and a gentleman, a churchwarden, with a wife who did charitable works. Then, turning towards me and calling me "Corporal Moon", he said a number of unpleasant and entirely unnecessary things about my own domestic arrangements. As I rose to respond, I was pre-empted by Rita who, furious, hit Saxby. While my opposition to violence and my preference for civilized debate is well known, nevertheless I could not but applaud as, indeed, did the audience at the time, although this despicable descent to gutter politics cast a shadow over my campaign.

The next day, Harriet informed me that Stanley had suffered a traumatic experience. He and some of his friends had been playing in Victoria Park, and had encountered a man who exposed himself to them – a 'flasher', in vulgar parlance. Stanley was visiting my mother when Saxby came canvassing, and Stanley insisted that Saxby was the man he had seen. My mother informed the police, and Saxby was arrested. Naturally,

Harriet was impatient with these notions and, in true Socialist style and in a genuinely sisterly way, she told me to stop mucking about and get into bed

this new sensation quite put Rita's assault in the shade, and I was heartened by the response as I continued canvassing, bearing a copy of the *Hackney Gazette* with news of the Saxby case prominently displayed on the front page. In fact, Stanley had made an unfortunate mistake. The real 'flasher' was found, who unaccountably bore no physical resemblance to my opponent, and Saxby was exonerated. At the election count, Saxby accused me of what are now known as dirty tricks, declaring in a quite unpardonable manner that I was devious and underhand. I ignored this vulgar abuse, and was declared the winner by a very satisfactory majority.

As I was celebrating, a man pushed his way through the throng. It was Herbert Morrison himself, my local MP, a government minister, and one of the great Labour figures of the century. He shook my hand. "Well done, Moon," he said, words that have resonated in my mind down the years.

And so, in the year of 1946, I stood on the threshold of a career which was then beyond my wildest dreams. To be a Councillor was the pinnacle of my ambition. I would devote my life to the good people of Down's Ward, I would serve them to the best of my ability, and beyond. No matter would be too mundane, no problem too great for me to tackle. The people had spoken and I, Harvey Moon, would listen.

CHAPTER TWO

THE FAMILY MOON

𝔊𝔞

I F I AM ANYTHING, I AM A FAMILY MAN. Long before the Tories tried to claim
that they were the party of family values, and then put their boasts into practice
by producing so-called love children on a production line of sleaze, I stood four-
square behind the old East End tradition of sticking to the family through thick
and thin, sharing the ups and the downs, celebrating together, mourning together,
supporting one another in a truly Socialist way. As a great-grandfather, I look with
pride on the new Moons who are carrying on the name I bear and to which I have
added, in a small way, some distinction.[6] I imbibed these values with my mother's milk,
and I feel I should now devote a few lines to myself as a son and a father.

My mother Violet, the Duchess as I used to call her, Nan to the family, was a
formidable woman. Although her gruff exterior hid a heart of gold, she did not suffer
fools lightly, and while her life had its tragedies, she always looked on the bright side.
Rather than telling her life story (because this, after all, is my life story), let me dip
into the bran tub of memories and see what comes forth. 'Get on with it, Harvey,' I
can hear her say. 'You always like to use four words where one would do.'

Right then, mum. I hope you'll forgive me for telling this tale, which I omitted from

6. On my ennoblement, I was approached by a genealogist who offered to research the family origins. Moon,
he told me, was a corruption of the Mesopotamian Ma'oun, meaning Mother of Oon (a minor deity noted for
sporting prowess). The Ma'oun dynasty of merchants moved westward, intermarrying as they went, settling
finally in France where they became assimilated in Normandy under the name of Moeun. Moving to England
during the Norman conquest, they settled on Hackney Marshes, where they established a thriving animal waste
business, providing fertiliser to the nobility, and also indulged in the distillation of crude spirit, hence the term
'moonshine'. Extracted from *The Moons in History*, Bespoke Family Trees of Chingford Ltd.

Opposite: *Mum off
on her honeymoon
after her second
marriage*

my previous volume due to a – perhaps unnecessary – sense of decorum. As I have said, my mother was a ladies' maid. She worked for a family called Cunningham, specifically Miss Edith Cunningham, in the years after the Great War. She never talked much about those days, so it was a shock when a letter came addressed to Mrs V.P. Moon. She didn't get letters, and was a bit flustered; indeed, she had to drink a cup of tea before she opened it. The letter was from a solicitor, telling her that she was the sole beneficiary in Miss Edith's will. Well, this was December 1946, and times were hard. A legacy could have transformed our lives. So I went with her to see the solicitor, me in my demob suit, her in her Sunday best. The Cunninghams had been wealthy, no doubt about it, and we were both, I think, making plans.

The solicitor soon set us to rights. Miss Edith, he said, had converted her assets into an annuity, which lapsed at death. I could see mum bridle a bit; had we come all this way on a wild goose chase? But no, there was an inheritance, and the solicitor took us outside to see it – an old Armstrong-Siddeley car. It was beautiful, right enough, but what use was it? I didn't drive, and more to the point, mum didn't drive. So the solicitor had to take us home in it, which caused a bit of a sensation in Stamford Hill, I can tell you.

Mum's first thought was that she should take driving lessons, and she wouldn't be talked out of it, so our landlady, who could drive, suggested that we should all go for a trip back to the Cunninghams' old house in the country and that Mum could have a go. She took the wheel on the way, but fortunately the butcher's boy was all right, and his bike wasn't too badly damaged.

It turned out that the house was now occupied by the military, so we went for a walk to the local church. Mum came over all funny in the graveyard, and something, to this day I don't know what, made me ask the vicar for the parish registers. I could see her through the window, standing over a grave and wiping away tears. It turned out that she had experienced what happened to so many ladies' maids in those days: seduction by the young man of the house. Mr Edgar had had his way with her, and she had given birth to a little girl who, sadly, died of measles while he was serving in France. He died at Ypres. After that, mum turned more religious. And, if you're wondering what happened to the car, it broke down and we sold it to a dealer for a few pounds.

I have beside me one of mum's scrapbooks, something she kept secret from us all, and which was only found after she died. Her room was strictly private, and it was surprising what we turned up after she had gone. She kept all sorts of things – my letters from India, my press cuttings, family photographs. There were some old postcards from Edgar Cunningham, wrapped up in red ribbon inside an envelope with a dried rose and some lavender petals. And a poem which mum had obviously written. It's not art of course, but it's part of our family story, and I reproduce it here.

A Ladies' Maid

I am a ladies' maid who serves
The rich folk and their guests
It's Violet this, and Violet that
And Violet, have this pressed

Opposite: *The somewhat extended Moon family*

I am only a name to them
A face about the house,
I am not quite a person
But I am not quite a mouse

Yet there's a man who loves me
Though his love he dare not show,
He is my darling E—
And I love my E—so

If we both shared the same estate
His wife he says he'd make me,
Although I am a ladies' maid
He swears he won't forsake me.

I pray that God will smile on him
When he goes to the War
And bring him safe back to my arms
From France's foreign shore.

It brings a lump to my throat to read it; a tragic example of how the working classes have been exploited through the generations. My poor old mum! So let me remember her in happier times.

If anyone was an unlikely celebrity, it was Mrs Violet Moon, but she had her five minutes of fame (as Stanley's friend Andy Warhol used to say) in Coronation Year, 1953. As with so many strange events of our lives, it was my old RAF colleague Lou Lewis (of whom more later) who was responsible. Mum was very much a Light Programme listener, although she took the news on the Home Service. So when Lou came home to say he had tickets for Michael Miles's *Take Your Pick* on Radio Luxembourg, she had no idea what he was talking about. 'What's *Take Your Pick*,' she asked, 'a play about Irish navvies?' We explained that it was a quiz show, and Lou was extremely excited, since he was convinced that he would win. He asked if we would test him on the 'Yes–No' interlude, a section of the entertainment in which neither of those words should be used. 'What words?' asked mum. 'Those words which I just mentioned,' said Lou. 'You said lots of words,' mum told him, that familiar twinkle coming into her eye. 'The words I used to describe the interlude,' said Lou impatiently. 'Oh,' said mum, 'you mean yes and no?' Yes, said Lou. 'Bonggg!' said I.

On many occasions in my life I have willingly placed duty before pleasure, and so it was on the night of the broadcast. Much as I would have wished to join my family in the delightful surroundings of the Hackney Empire, I put the interests of my constituents first, as was my invariable practice. However, since the evening entered family folklore, I can picture the scene as if I had been there myself, Lou and my mother on the stage with some other hopefuls, my mother particularly noticeable since she had broken her ankle and was ensconced in a wheelchair, her leg in plaster causing something of a hazard to those trying to move about the stage.

Lou was the first contestant. Mr Miles informed him that the clock had started, and asked Lou if he could hear it. Lou, his attention more on the audience than on the compère, said yes. The gong tolled its doleful message. My mother came next. To every question, she answered steadfastly, 'Mind your own business,' varying it occasionally with a firm 'Mind your own.' The audience was transported. This was entertainment of the highest order. She had beaten the clock! Then the time came to choose between accepting money or opening a box that might contain a prize of significant value. Doughty in her wheelchair, my mother dismissed the first offer of half a crown and the second offer of five shillings. Michael Miles increased the temptation, moving from one to two guineas. As is traditional, half of the audience exhorted my mother to take the money, while the other half wished her to open the box. Such appeals to greed throw into focus the system under which we live, a capitalist version of the bread and circuses offered by the Roman emperors as a distraction to their people. But such considerations were, of course, far from my mother's mind as, encouraged by the applause, she cogitated on her fateful decision.

Mum in her wheelchair at the Hackney Empire

I have been suspicious of the feasibility of obtaining something for nothing since taking the advice of the late Robert Maxwell to invest in six dozen cases of the finest vintage claret which, he assured me, could be sold for a sum far in excess of the pittance he was asking. When the time came to sell the wine, Maxwell informed me that the importers, Hoch Hock (Cayman) Ltd, had gone bankrupt, that the wine now belonged to the liquidators, and that my money could not be refunded. This was the first of my dealings with the man, and should have guided me in my future relations with him. However, I invariably think the best of people, and I confess that his generous hospitality, his kindness in inviting me to cruise in the Mediterranean on his yacht with its attractive crew of young female research assistants, and the more than satisfactory emoluments that he offered merely for printing my name at the top of various letterheads, somewhat veiled my eyes to his true nature. As the old saying goes, you don't get owt for nowt, and the incident of the Memoirs brought this home to me with considerable strength.

Back to my mother! Lou, who was still on the stage, insisted that she open the box. He said he had worked out scientifically that the prize would be worth more than the two guineas that Michael Miles was offering. My mother, who should have known better, took Lou's advice. It was fortunate for him that she was in a wheelchair, since her prize was a pair of roller skates. Even under normal circumstances the

likelihood of my old mum taking to wheels was zero – talk about a traffic hazard! As it was, she could have won nothing more unsuitable, apart perhaps from a set of peek-a-boo underwear.

Other memories flood back. My mother sitting in a Soho nightclub, wearing her black coat and clutching her handbag, not wanting to be mistaken for a lady of the night. My mother shedding a tear over the death of Queen Mary. My mother expressing her pride at my not inconsiderable achievements. My mother in her hospital bed with, as she put it, plaster up to her gusset and a bedpan to cope with, later dismissing us with the announcement that she had been given something for her bowels and urgent attention was necessary. She was a trouper, my mum, as traditional as the roast beef of old England, a woman who lived through history, an unsung heroine who, all unknowing, wiped the bottom of a Lord. Truly, we will not see her like again.

Of course, in the difficult family circumstances which, thanks to my former wife Rita, we were forced to confront, my mother was not just a mother to me; she was a typical salt-of-the-earth surrogate mother and nan to my children Stanley and Margaret.

Stanley was always a bright lad, an imp with a sense of mischief. Scamp was my mother's name for him when he was small. His many fans will, of course, have read his autobiography,[7] but this deals primarily with his years of celebrity, omitting much of family interest. Indeed, if I did not know him better, I would believe that the celebrated Hollywood director was ashamed of his humble origins, so I feel some responsibility to set the record straight and offer here some vignettes as a loving father as well as a social historian.

Young Stan got into the usual childhood scrapes, but he was always self-reliant; for example, he was evacuated to the countryside during the war, but made his own way back to London. He was also blessed, even at an early age, with a fertile imagination. I did my bit to get him into grammar school when his 11-plus results were borderline, but Stanley himself tipped the balance during his interview with the Headmaster. The little terror told the Head that I had been engaged in secret work during the war, and had achieved the rank of Wing Commander! When Stanley confessed, my first instinct was, as always, to tell the truth. On mature consideration, however, I felt it better to let Stanley's version stand, for after all, what is a tiny white lie when it is set against a deeper, more essential truth? My war work was as valuable as if I had been a secret agent and an officer, and Stanley's small embroidery was surely harmless.

Some, of course, may be more concerned that I, a lifelong believer in and doughty battler for equality of opportunity, should send my son to a grammar school. As I argued at the time, and would maintain today, by paying for Stanley's education[8] I created a vacancy within the excellent state system from which another child would

It was an era when the older man fared better than the younger, even though, try as I might, I never came to terms with the intricacies of corsetry

---

7. *Moon Over Hollywood*, Stanley Moon as told to Barry Lemoto, Scribner's.
8. To be entirely accurate, I made occasional contributions when I could afford them, while Rita bore the brunt of the payments, but this in no sense invalidates the principle involved.

Opposite: *Stanley at Stanmore in 1953*

The three terrors;
Derek, Stanley
and Roy

doubtless benefit. I am pleased that the modern Labour Party appears to have adopted this eminently sensible view.

Having dismissed the usual childhood ambitions of being a pilot, a train-driver or a footballer, Stanley finally found a niche as a draughtsman in an engineering factory drawing office. He found it rather dull, and thus went uncomplainingly to do his duty as a National Serviceman in my old outfit, the RAF. There he developed the two interests that were to dominate his life – photography and women.

'Treat every woman as if she is your mum,' I told him as he set off on the train to Stanmore, forgetting for the moment that his mother was not the paragon of virtue which my advice was intended to imply. But of course, boys will be boys and girls will be girls, although the 1950s were rather more straitlaced in terms of opportunity than is the case today. It was an era when the older man fared better than the younger, even though, try as I might, I never came to terms with the intricacies of corsetry. Stanley, as a young and then unmarried man,[9] felt nature's siren call, and he spent

---

9. Stanley's six marriages have led to a recurring family joke on the occasions when we speak. Me: 'Any new daughters-in-law to report son?' Stanley: 'Oh, give it a rest, dad!' I have always been possessed of a sparkling sense of humour.

many hours discussing the urgent nature of his quest with his friends Derek and Roy. As for myself, I am lucky to have been blessed with unusual self-control when it comes to the distaff department. I never, to employ a euphemism, 'went into town' when stationed in Poona, satisfying myself with the most up-to-date copy of *Lilliput*, which often wrote on sporting matters, and studying the most efficacious techniques of dribbling and shooting alone in my bunk.

Stanley's attempts to become a man in the most complete sense of the word seemed always to lead him into difficulties. There was, for example, a nurse called Marjorie, a young woman with a certain reputation for generous ways; in the hearty male atmosphere of the NAAFI she was reputed to "go like a rocket". To my son, she appeared the answer to a young man's prayer. Eager, perhaps over-eager to impress, he plied her with Babycham (then viewed as a particularly sophisticated and ladylike drink), and pressed her for a date. As we laughed about it later, during one of our father-to-son conversations, free of embarrassment on both sides, young Stanley confessed to feeling downcast when Marjorie said she had a boyfriend. With true Moon tenacity, Stanley pressed his suit, and Marjorie conceded that she might be free on Sunday when her boyfriend played football.

At some grave personal risk Stanley, who was by then a driver in the Stanmore car pool, agreed to meet her in a Humber staff car. Filled with anticipation, his hair heavily Brylcreemed, Stanley was there at the appointed time, eager for his initiation into the mysterious rites of manhood. Marjorie, though, had some astounding news. She wished to visit St Albans to see the cathedral. On church parade, the words of the padre about resisting sordid desire had touched her heart; she felt she had been cheapening herself.

Stanley was quick to reassure her, stating that her generosity was widely held to be invaluable, but Marjorie was adamant. A sightseeing trip was all that was on offer, since it would be impossible to fall from the straight and narrow on consecrated ground. Thoroughly disgruntled, Stanley, who had always intended to smuggle her out of the base in the car boot, resolved that she should stay there far longer than was necessary.

"Did I do wrong dad?" he asked me, anxious for fatherly reassurance. "The Lord knows, son," I replied, with one of those sallies of wit for which I have been renowned throughout my public life.

In due course, Stanley tried again. This time the circumstances were more propitious. A casual encounter with Marjorie revealed that she had abandoned her ambition of entering a nunnery for, as she told him, you're only young once. She agreed to a date, and Stanley brought his camera, encouraging her into a positive frame of mind by comparing her with film stars of the day, and telling Marjorie that she should apply to the Rank Charm School. From the photographs, I would judge Marjorie to have been a rather homely girl but all is fair in love and war, as they say. Unfortunately, their trysting spot was close to the base, and Stanley's attention was diverted by an unusual aeroplane noise. While Marjorie pouted, he aimed his camera at a Vulcan

Stanley was there at the appointed time, eager for his initiation into the mysterious rites of manhood

Stanley with the notorious Marjorie

bomber which was coming in to land. Since it was on the secret list, security was high, and my hapless son was arrested on suspicion of being a Communist spy.[10]

Stanley's next escapade involved his family. Soho was far from my usual stamping grounds at the time, but in the cause of solidarity with an old RAF comrade who had found a job with a jazz band I had made my way there, accompanied by my mother and by Rita, who was naturally at home in that milieu. Unbeknownst to us, Stanley was also in the 'sinful square mile' with his friends, who had determined that he should not be demobbed without tasting the pleasures of the flesh. Derek had undertaken to arrange an encounter with a lady of the town. Roy, who was engaged, expressed his disapproval, but loyally accompanied his friends to share in Stanley's rite of passage. While Stanley sought Dutch courage in beer, Derek went on a reconnaissance mission, returning with the news that he had negotiated successfully with a young woman somewhat resembling a cinematic heroine of the time, the Peek-a-Boo Girl, Veronica Lake.

As Stanley and Roy approached her, the girl, pardonably confused, took Roy to be her appointed companion and led him, somewhat intimately, to her boudoir in

---

10. Mention of Communism leads me to refute the baseless accusations made by Mr Boris Godunovski in his scurrilous book, *Agents of Influence* (Coldwater Press, Langley, Virginia). In it, the former KGB agent wrote: "I entertained the Burslem MP, Harry Moon, at the Gay Hussar. It was obvious that Moon was a man of no influence whatsoever, and I recall the dinner only because my expenses were queried by Moscow Centre." In fact Mr Godunovski's profession was quite evident, and I made it my business, while accepting his hospitality, to give him no information of any kind. I quite properly reported this contact to our own security service, which failed to treat it with the gravity it deserved. "What on earth could you tell the Russians, Harvey?" was not, I believe, an adequate response to the attempted subversion of a leading Member of Parliament.

Meard Street, leaving a crestfallen Stanley to return to the pub. However, when Roy returned after a short interval, Stanley was encouraged to take his place. It was at the moment of his triumphant exit from the shabby little house, a man at last, that he was confronted by his father, his mother and his grandmother on their way home.

We looked at each other in silence for a moment, the red light burning accusingly in the window behind him. 'What are you doing round here, son,' I asked, perhaps foolishly. 'Just getting some snapshots developed,' he replied.

This tale, redolent of the period and the pre-permissive days of the 1950s, seems to me a charming curio, and I cannot understand why Stanley omitted it from his book.

Snapshots were once more to lead Stanley into difficulties, but since they were the foundation of his subsequent career I again feel sure that he will not object to my telling the tale. The girl concerned here was Dilys, a true *femme fatale*, and one somewhat out of my son's league at the time, although his promotion through the divisions was rapid. After leaving the RAF, Stanley returned to the drawing office albeit without any great enthusiasm, and found Dilys still working there. He remembered her clearly (she had what the writers of a certain kind of fiction used to call 'a generous bust', and a penchant for angora sweaters which displayed them to their best advantage), although her recollections of him were less clear. She was clearly interested in the new, more mature Stanley, who gave the impression, without going into detail, that his National Service had involved rather more than being a driver. Dilys said that her ambition was to live in Paris on the Left Bank, and to become an air stewardess. Stanley was impressed with such worldliness and invited her to his demob party, where Dilys created something of a sensation. Even I, burdened as I was at the time with political affairs, noticed her. It was at the party that Dilys told Stanley she wanted men to be attracted by her mind rather than her body. Stanley diplomatically said it was possible to admire them both.

After that they frequently had lunch together in the drawing office, sharing Dilys's sandwiches, or taking walks in the park. She developed her dreams of a glamorous life, becoming an existentialist muse in Paris, befriending Jean-Paul Sartre and Simone de Beauvoir, singing with Juliette Greco, and so on, while Stanley revealed his dream of becoming a professional photographer.

Thus when they found themselves the last to leave on a Saturday morning, the conversation turned naturally to photography. Stanley had joined a camera club, and sought Dilys's opinion on what he should submit to the Hackney Wildlife section of the club competition. His preference was for Charlie Harris's ferrets, which were trained to kill rats for sport on Saturday mornings. This offended Dilys's female sensibilities, and she changed the subject, asking if Stanley ever did portraits. Stanley said he did, if the sitter looked like Olivia de Haviland and was prepared to undertake a saucy pose. Chancing his arm, he declared that every serious photographer should have his portrait, his still-life, his action shot … and his nude. Dilys, twirling her glasses, asked Stanley if he was a serious photographer. Naturally he said he was very serious, and regarded photography as an art form.

It was the word 'art' that apparently spoke to the soul of Dilys, who volunteered surprisingly quickly to remove her clothes for some serious nude studies. The venue was a problem but, since she had the office keys, she suggested that the session should take place there and then. Young Stan, agog, rushed home for his camera.

Despite one or two shaky and unfocused shots, the pictures turned out well, pleasing both photographer and sitter. Stanley presented Dilys with a set as a souvenir, and somehow managed to forget his camera when it came to further encounters. Dilys did not seem to mind. Having taken his ferret picture along to the club and pinned it up with the other wildlife photographs, albeit without any great hopes of winning, Stanley was amazed to reach the exhibition and see a lively crowd around his picture with his boss from the drawing office, Mr Ives, at the centre. Pushing his way through, Stanley was even more amazed to see Dilys's ample charms where he had expected to see ferrets.

Stanley's ferret study. Sadly it never made it to the Hackney Wildlife section of his camera club's competition

Ives ripped the offending photograph from the display, confronting Stanley in a gibbering fit of rage. 'My wife has visited that office,' he hissed, tearing the photograph to confetti. 'See me first thing tomorrow morning, Moon!'

It was an apprehensive Stanley who kept the appointment next day. Ives had recovered his composure, and said he would allow Stanley to keep his job under two conditions: first, that he wrote a letter of apology; second, that he handed over the remaining prints, and the negatives – all the negatives. Stanley told me that Ives was visibly slobbering at this point. When Stanley enquired about Dilys, Ives was adamant.

She was a slut who would be given a week's wages and fired on the spot. As Ives reached for further adjectives, Stanley took action, throwing a punch which he described as a real beauty. The blow drove Ives backwards, and he collapsed in an undignified heap in the wastepaper basket, within which his rear-quarters remained securely lodged.

After that, there was little to say. Dilys bade Stanley a fond farewell, confessing that she had switched the photographs because, as she said, he had managed to capture her reality. She thought she might go back to Paris for a while, or again approach BOAC about becoming a stewardess. She wished Stanley luck, and disappeared from his life, or so it seemed then. For Dilys, the world appeared to be her oyster. For Stanley, there was the bleak prospect of no job, no income, and apparently unachievable dreams of becoming the next Cecil Beaton or Karsh of Ottawa. In moments of crisis, I always reach for an appropriate piece of wisdom. Never mind, son, I told the disconsolate Stan. Something will turn up.

Let me now turn to my daughter Margaret, the comfort of my old age, the apple of my eye, the sunshine of my life. Now, bless her, she's the image of her old nan; but behind the grey hair I can see the chubby blonde teenager who welcomed me back from the war. It is a privilege to tell at least part of her story, for behind every successful man there is a woman, and Margaret has been the woman to stand most often behind me, the chatelaine of Moon Mansion, as I jokingly refer to this humble abode.

Margaret's story is inextricably entwined with that of her late husband, Lou Lewis, or Archibald Barnardo Lewis, to give him his full name. On our return from Poona, Lou gave me to understand that he was looking forward to a warm welcome back into the bosom of his family. Later, I found him alone in a pub, where he confessed his secret. There was no family. He had been abandoned as a baby in a shopping bag outside Joe Lyons in the Seven Sisters Road, and raised an orphan. Naturally I invited him to stay temporarily with mum and me, thus becoming his honorary father and later – although this was not an unmixed blessing – his father-in-law.

Margaret and Rita in the Tottenham prefab

For Margaret, then working at a factory that manufactured prophylactics ('the johnny factory' as it was universally known), it was love at first sight, as it was for my old comrade. Love, they say, is blind, and so it was here. Lou, never blessed with enormous strength of character nor with a highly developed intelligence, was possessed of a sweet nature and was easily led. Hence when he unwittingly became involved with the redoubtable criminal figure of Conny Rosenthal, a notorious spiv, it was hard to be angry. Many's the time a lecture sprang to my lips, only to die stillborn as I forced down a mouthful of black market sausage. My principles were offended, but in difficult times the welfare of my mother took precedence and I tolerated Lou's peccadilloes for the sake of the family.

The saga of Lou and Margaret, fictionalized in the 1960s by one of my former daughters-in-law,[11] was a somewhat highly-flavoured account of their early years, coloured by Stanley's vivid imagination, then in the grip of mind-expanding drugs of inferior quality. Since my own name was linked with this farrago,[12] and since I offered a dignified silence at the time, I think it only right to set out briefly here the story of their courtship and subsequent marriage.

To Maggie, bored by her work and dreaming of a career as an actress, Lou appeared a glamorous figure. He had money. He could procure those items that were in short supply. He had the use of Conny Rosenthal's car. She was prepared to overlook the

---

11. Ellen Di Mambro Moon, *Hoodlum*, Ace Books.
12. 'Harry Sun and Harvey Moon – Are They Related?', *Private Eye*, 29 September 1966. This article treated Ellen Di Mambro's novel as a work of truth rather than of fiction, and its author sought to discredit me at a time when I was engaged in a bitter struggle with the left-wing in Burslem. The magazine's attempts to link me with the Kray twins was manifest nonsense. Naturally, as a mover and shaker in the 1960s I had met the brothers at various sporting and social events, and participated in some convivial charity evenings at their Knightsbridge club, Esmeralda's Barn, but the late Ron Kray and I had rather different recreational tastes.

shady associations for the benefits they brought, and failed entirely to see that Lou's function was essentially that of a messenger-boy.

Poor Lou was one of those people on whom nature delights to play practical jokes. When Rosenthal asked him to collect some cases of smuggled Irish whiskey, Lou drove trustingly to a warehouse in the docks, became hopelessly lost, and was observed trying to make his getaway by a passing policeman. The policeman watched, first with amusement and then with suspicion, as Lou tried this road and that, always ending up in front of the law. Lou was arrested and charged with being in possession of the whiskey, as well as driving without a licence. I volunteered to stand surety.

Margaret was naturally distraught, and foolishly consented to take a farewell drive with Lou on the night before the trial. With the bad luck that often attended him, the car broke down in an isolated spot, forcing Lou and Margaret to spend the night together. Had it been anyone else, a convenient breakdown in a wood might have seemed to be the product of forethought. Lou's intellectual ability was not capable of such an imaginative leap. Fortune smiled in one sense, since the young lovers huddled together for warmth and nature took its course.

To Maggie, bored by her work and dreaming of a career as an actress, Lou appeared a glamorous figure

Lou arrived in court at the crucial moment, and was sentenced to three months in Wormwood Scrubs. Margaret was deeply upset, the more so when she thought that she was pregnant. Her mother was typically unsympathetic, suggesting an abortion. The wretched girl turned to me for fatherly solace. I took the opportunity to utter a few well-chosen words on the topic of responsibility, pointing out that, having been brought up by Rita, Margaret had obviously been subject to malign influence. Surprisingly, these words did not comfort her. Resolved to have the baby and to marry Lou, Margaret was again deeply upset when it transpired that she was not pregnant after all. As long as I live, I shall never understand women!

On his release, Lou determined to 'go straight', and spoke enthusiastically of becoming a farmer in Tanganyika, an occupation for which he had neither aptitude nor experience. Margaret, ever loyal, said she would accompany him, and Lou asked me to furnish a reference. Ever a man for plain-speaking and never one to shirk his duty, I informed the authorities of Lou's prison record, and his application was refused. You may say that this was harsh, that I might perhaps have modified the truth in some way, but from time to time a man must be saved from himself.

Despondent and homeless after the destruction of Ladysmith Dwellings when an unexploded bomb unexpectedly exploded, Lou and I shared the most uncomfortable quarters in a lodging-house in Wells Street. Since he was always something of a hypochondriac, none of us took Lou seriously when he complained of feeling unwell. I myself was hardly the picture of health, despite my robust constitution and essentially optimistic nature. Determined to find a home and to marry, Lou and Margaret were going door-to-door in search of rooms when Lou suffered a worse than usual coughing fit, found that his handkerchief was red with blood, and fainted.

Opposite: Margaret in a very fetching tam-o-shanter

We wept as a family when the unfortunate orphan was diagnosed as having

tuberculosis, and despatched to a sanatorium in Aberdeen.

Life seemed bleak indeed. Margaret resolved to devote her life to the service of the sick, enrolling in the St John's Ambulance Brigade. After her training, she was entrusted with the care of supporters at White Hart Lane, home to Tottenham Hotspur Football Club. As a supporter of Spurs' arch rivals, the Arsenal, I felt that her talents might have been more usefully deployed elsewhere.

She then enrolled as a trainee nurse at Hackney Hospital, though her career there was short-lived, an independent spirit and a liking for nail-varnish affronting the authorities.

Unemployed, and missing her "blue eyes", Margaret was at her most vulnerable when I received a letter from Lou with devastating news. He had met a nurse called Morag McDonald and had fallen deeply in love. In a postscript, he said that he was getting better. Debating with myself over how best to break the news to my darling Margaret, I became abstracted and blurted out the information somewhat insensitively. As Margaret dissolved in tears, I put a fatherly arm around her shoulder, murmuring words of comfort. I recall that I told her there were plenty of fish in the sea, but she remained inconsolable.

In all charity, it can be said that Veronica made Lou appear like Einstein

In her hour of need, Margaret turned for solace to her friend Veronica Spicer. In all charity, it can be said that Veronica made Lou appear like Einstein. A plain, plump girl with a lazy eye, which meant that one side of her spectacles was covered with sticking plaster, Veronica had the rare gift of being intrusive, insensitive and aggravating, while thinking herself the opposite. In many ways, she had all the qualifications to become a successful Member of Parliament. Margaret's patience and understanding were frequently put to the test, but she would brook no criticism of her friend.

Abandoned by the love of her life, Margaret kept a small flame alive for Lou while exploring other possibilities. Men came and went. I recall Lionel the tailor; Tom the descendant of Indian royalty, who shamefully abandoned her; Alfie the boxer, who refused to give up boxing. She worked in a hat shop, then trained as a hair stylist and went to work in her mother's business. Out of the blue, a letter came from Aberdeen, written on lined paper in Lou's distinctive, unformed hand. He made no mention of Morag, but talked about his health, which was still improving, and about the old days with Margaret. She wrote back, saying that if he was ever in London it would be nice to see him. Lou took the next train south, arriving at the maisonette where my mother and I were now living, with a small suitcase and a hopeful expression. Naturally we took him in, and the young lovers resumed their relationship, although both had changed. Margaret was more forceful, more experienced in life. Lou, with a damaged lung, saw himself as a semi-invalid and avoided the slightest exertion. 'Old soldier' are the words which spring immediately to mind. Eventually he found a job as a junior salesman in the shoe department of Burgess's and the sound of wedding bells was again in the air.

Margaret had always been slightly resentful that Veronica had been married before her because Margaret, blonde, vivacious and attractive appeared much more of a catch than her friend. Veronica's tale seemed typical of her. On an outing from the

johnny factory, Veronica had got drunk and been taken advantage of. When she discovered she was pregnant her father threw her out, and she went to live in Rita's prefab with Margaret and Stanley. Despite her best efforts, Veronica could not remember with whom she had enjoyed, if that is the word, her romantic encounter. By chance, she and Margaret met their former colleague, Ian, and Veronica remembered. Ian, whose mental equipment was not dissimilar to Veronica's, fainted on being told that he was to be a father, and it was Margaret who suggested that marriage might be in order – the thought had not occurred to him. Ian immediately proposed, and they moved to Welwyn Garden City. I had not seen Veronica since then, but we were all bracing ourselves for her return as Margaret's matron of honour on the day when she would finally become Mrs Lewis.

Veronica and Margaret pretend to be the Andrews Sisters

CHAPTER THREE

FRAILTY, THY NAME WAS RITA

THOSE WHO ENTER PUBLIC LIFE must be prepared for the slings and arrows of outrageous fortune to be aimed in their direction. He who mounts the platform must ever be prepared for the trapdoor to open under his feet. Or, to put it another way, each man must bear his own cross. In my long career, as I reached for and won the glittering prizes, clawing my way with great sensitivity and concern for others to the top of the greasy pole, I had a cross. Her name was Rita. She was my wife. As the discerning reader will have gathered, I like to think I am a man with broad shoulders and a generous heart. Throughout my career in politics, during which, in the immortal words of the Bard, I did the state some service,[13] I was noted for a total lack of pomposity and a willingness to roll up my shirtsleeves and muck in with the best of them.

'Big-hearted Harvey' was my slogan in the election year of 1979, when I held Burslem with a majority of three after six re-counts. My ennoblement in Mrs Thatcher's first Honours List, with a subsequent Conservative win in the by-election, was seen

---

13. I would recall particularly my responsibility for providing the beer and sandwiches which featured in so many discussions at No. 10 Downing Street during Harold Wilson's premiership; the honour which I felt when I was dubbed the washer-up in Harold Wilson's kitchen cabinet; my frequent appearances as linesman during football matches between the Lords and the Commons; my membership of parliamentary delegations to Bermuda, the Bahamas, Jamaica, Barbados, St Lucia, St Kitts, Gstaad, Davos, Klosters, etc., and my consultancy to the Tourist Authority of the Maldives; my time as Robert Maxwell's deputy during the period when he was in charge of catering in the House of Commons; and the many occasions on which I 'caught the Speaker's eye' to make cogent interventions on Bills ranging from the Local Authorities (Miscellaneous Provisions) Bill of 1964, to the Local Authorities (Further Miscellaneous Provisions) Bill of 1967 (see the relevant issues of *Hansard* and Volume 1 of these Memoirs for extended coverage of these vital matters).

Opposite: *Rita on a bed, which seems appropriate*

by some as a cynical Tory ploy. I preferred to regard it as a just reward for my years of devoted service, despite the pressure on me from party colleagues to refuse the honour. The full story must wait for a further volume. However, since I was at the time a figure of some controversy, my long-divorced wife sought to blacken my reputation by approaching the *News of the World* and providing material for three pages of lies, half-truths and distortions.[14] Naturally I took legal advice, but I was informed by a representative of Lord Goodman that a court case might well go against me since the material was so cleverly written. Now, I feel, is an appropriate moment dispassionately to set the record straight about Rita, who recently passed away. The fact that the dead cannot be libelled has obviously played no part in my decision.

I was an innocent young lad, and she was a woman already experienced in the ways of the world

We first met when I was an innocent young lad, and she was a woman already experienced in the ways of the world. She was obviously attracted by my athleticism, my footballing prowess, my dashing style and my sense of humour. To be honest, I was flattered. And so, waiting for a bus in a shelter on Hackney Marshes, I acceded to her urgent requests in what was a rather brief encounter. Four months later we were married; four months after that Margaret was born, followed six years later by Stanley.

Married life turned me into an early example of a 'new man', an expert in changing nappies and in housework. At Rita's urging, I willingly played my part about the house, and although I invariably believed her when Rita said she was going to have one of her frequent 'nights out with the girls', I see in retrospect that even then the love of a good and honest man was not enough for her.

When I volunteered to do my duty for King and Empire, I suggested that Rita might involve herself in one of the voluntary services. Informing me that her services were always given voluntarily, she took a job as a barmaid at the White Bear in Coventry Street, leaving Margaret and my mother to concern themselves with the welfare of young Stan. He told me on my return from India that he had experienced a succession of transatlantic 'uncles' throughout the war years, and was at first downcast when I was unable to provide the 'candy' and tinned pineapple chunks to which he had become accustomed. Even now, my blood boils when I think of the sweet innocence of youth besmirched by the red-headed houri to whom I had given the proud name of Moon.

In the immediate post-war period, Rita was adamant in her refusal to pick up the threads of married life, but my hopes of returning her to the straight and narrow path of propriety were raised when I received an urgent summons to visit her. I found her in a darkened room, with a bruised face and puffy eyes; she had been attacked by the first of her post-war lovers, one Clifford, a trumpeter in the orchestra of the London Palladium. Setting aside our differences, I comforted Rita in her hour of need, during which I was interrupted by the arrival of the woman beater himself. We had a sharp confrontation in which, drawing on the combat skills I had learned in the RAF, I put him to flight, sustaining only bruised knuckles and a slightly blackened

---

14. The headline read: 'Hypocrite Harvey, Lord of the Chance'.

eye in the process. Rita's employment of a well-directed stiletto heel played a small part in the incident.

Emboldened by Rita's penitence, I returned immediately to Ladysmith Dwellings, packed a suitcase and went back to the prefab, prepared to let bygones be bygones. On my arrival, Margaret informed me that Rita had disguised her bruises with make-up and gone to a tea dance. Declaring that the woman was beyond redemption, I went home to my mother. But as time went by and my temper cooled, I again dreamed of a reconciliation. Despite her lack of concern about my feelings, despite her high-handed ways, despite everything, a flame still burned in my heart, hard though Rita tried to blow it out.

Rita's next involvement was with the criminal empire of Conny Rosenthal and his henchman Monty Fish. While my young friend Lou was an unknowing pawn in the sinister Rosenthal's game, the more worldly Rita had no such excuse. That she should become manageress of Rosenthal's dubious establishment, The Pink Flamingo, was hardly surprising, nor was the fact that she should present the impressionable Stanley with yet another 'uncle' in Monty Fish, a vulgarian of the worst order, albeit with some redeeming features that will be dealt with in a subsequent chapter.

Concerned for Stanley, I managed to persuade Rosenthal that Monty might be better employed elsewhere, using the full force of my eloquence supported by the suggestion that, if Monty did not seek pastures new, I would prevail on Lou to implicate Rosenthal

Rita the glorified barmaid with my old sparring partner Monty Fish

in his court case. Rosenthal saw the logic of my argument, and despatched Monty to Liverpool. Hoping yet again for a reconciliation, I was again rebuffed, although I felt some grim satisfaction when Rosenthal sought to place his relationship with Rita on a more personal footing and felt the terrifying force of her anger.

One of nature's barmaids, Rita went to work at a hotel in Earls Court, where she was attracted by the silver tongue of a guest calling himself Squadron Leader Rupert Brooke. Never a literary woman, she found nothing strange in this name. Brooke invited her to spend a weekend with him in Bournemouth, an invitation which she naturally accepted with alacrity, but which she had to forgo when Lou was taken to hospital. She subsequently discovered that she had narrowly escaped an encounter with the notorious murderer Neville Heath, but even that could not interrupt her headlong career of debauchery.

Finding it impossible to exist without a man, even though a long-suffering, nay saintly candidate was waiting in the wings (I refer, of course, to myself), she resumed her affair with Monty who had returned from Liverpool after the arrest and conviction of Rosenthal. Never scrupulous about legality, she readily agreed to play hostess at gaming parties in the none-too-glamorous surroundings of her Tottenham prefab. There she met a man who was to have considerable importance in her life, Leo Brandon.

Rita was flattered when this wealthy, gentlemanly, silver-haired milliner, proprietor with his mother of Madame Phyllis of Holborn, invited her to the opera and the theatre. She convinced herself, with surprising naivety, that Leo was the man for whom she had been waiting all her life. Why, he was such a gentleman that he had never tried to lay a finger on her. Informing Monty of this in the course of a violent argument, during which she ejected him from the prefab and her life with the aid of a hot iron, Rita was shocked when Monty revealed that Leo was a homosexual. So, when I heard the news, was I. The man was always in and out of the prefab. He had taken Margaret on as a junior sales assistant. He was advising and, I learned later, financing Rita in a new business venture, a ladies' hairdressing establishment. He had befriended Stanley, my innocent young son, who was now seemingly at the mercy of a pervert. Could one be sure that he had not wormed his way into Rita's affections specifically because of Stan?

In those days, before homosexuals were 'gay', they were discreet. Leo Brandon neither minced nor lisped. Margaret, when she learned the truth, was revolted. My mother was more tolerant, believing that they should be castrated for their own good. To a man's man such as myself, a red-blooded, thoroughgoing Englishman and proud of it, there was only one course of action open to me – physical violence. In a state of hysterical rage, I went to confront Brandon, incoherently expressing my fears. To give him his due, he did not flinch.

'How many twelve-year-old girls have you molested this month, Harvey?' he enquired. The question stopped me in my tracks. I removed my hands from his throat. There could be but one answer. In later life, when confronted with others of the Brandon

She subsequently discovered that she had narrowly escaped an encounter with the notorious murderer Neville Heath

Opposite: *A study of Rita by Phelps of Hackney, who is noted for his retouching ability*

Rita snapped this picture of life at The Happy Curl

ilk, I remembered that afternoon and was always prepared to shake their hand (albeit making sure to wash mine afterwards at the first available opportunity).

It was with Brandon that Rita discovered an unexpected aptitude for ballroom dancing, and it was after one such occasion that Brandon encountered a young man from whom he had parted in acrimonious circumstances. The man, after being refused a reconciliation, accused Brandon of importuning, and he was charged with outraging public decency.

As a former solicitor's clerk and Justice of the Peace, I have always held the law in the highest esteem, and my campaign to bring back the birch was widely supported at the time,[15] but here was a manifest injustice. While I cannot condone Rita's actions, I can confess to some sneaking sympathy.[16]

At the trial, it was Brandon's word against that of his accuser. Things looked bleak – after all, what could be more suggestive of unnatural inclinations than millinery? Then Rita took to the witness stand. She told the court that she had spent many happy hours in Brandon's arms, a statement absolutely true in so far as it applied to ballroom dancing. Pressed by the prosecution she went further, announcing that, on her forthcoming divorce, she and Brandon intended to marry. When this statement was

15. I was honoured to be the sole Labour representative on the Burslem Backs the Birch Committee, chaired by the Dowager Lady Trollope, with Brigadier General Anthony Hinson (Retd.), the former Bishop of Bloemfontein, and the distinguished Burslem Sentinel leader writer and Scout correspondent, Ronnie Thwaites, among its membership.
16. For reasons which will later become clear, Rita was at the time seeking to divorce me - an obvious cry for help and attention.

greeted with scepticism, she declared, 'Well, I wouldn't marry a nancy boy, would I?' There was uproar in court, and the case was dismissed.

The rather bizarre relationship continued until Brandon was again accused of importuning, this time with more justification. Speaking personally, I have never seen the attractions of Hyde Park as a trysting place, although one supposes that Guardsmen may hold an appeal for those inclined towards the love that once dared not speak its name. Brandon was convicted and imprisoned. On his release, he moved to Tangier. His subsequent history is unknown.

The disappearance of Brandon chastened Rita, who devoted her energies to the hairdressing salon which he had assisted her to buy. At first a sleeping partner, Rita soon discovered that its owner, the eponymous Kitty, was prone to taking late lunches, dipping into the till when short of cash, and had a cavalier attitude towards her customers. Rita manoeuvred Kitty out, then encouraged Margaret to learn the trade and installed her as stylist. When two strong-minded women get together the sensible man takes cover, and my premonitions of trouble would be amply borne out. At the beginning of 1953, though, Margaret's thoughts were fixed firmly on her marriage to Lou Lewis, an event that, for a number of reasons, marked the beginning of a new chapter in the life of the Moon family.

My principles were clear and unequivocal: if an old comrade was in trouble, he must be helped

Our domestic arrangements at the time should perhaps be explained. My mother, Lou and I lived in a maisonette. Margaret lived with Rita, as did Stanley when he was on leave from the RAF. When Lou and Margaret married, Lou would move in with Rita, leaving a spare room in the maisonette on which Stanley had his eye.

One January night, on my return from work, my mother was cooking sausage rolls in preparation for what later came to be called a hen party. Her mind fixed on the wedding, she asked me whether I had organized a lucky chimney-sweep for the event – one of those delightful East End customs now sadly passed into abeyance. Our conversation was interrupted by the arrival of Lou who, ever one to draw attention to his damaged lung and fragile health, was breathing heavily. He asked me whether, in my capacity as a councillor, I could have something done about the stairs. I replied jocularly that I would have an escalator installed. Lou, whose mental state would have been highly prized among those who take part in transcendental meditation took me at my word and was briefly cheered.

Sighing heavily, he announced that he was going to bed after a rough day. A customer had come to the shoe department at Burgess's, sent him up the ladder a dozen times, tried on every pair of shoes in the place, and only bought a tin of dubbin. As he departed with the hangdog look so typical of him, my mother remarked (not for the first time) that she felt Margaret could have done better. I kept my own counsel.

The next day Lou was at home, packing for his imminent move and rehearsing his wedding speech, when the doorbell rang. Outside was a tall, thin black man in a thin suit, obviously suffering from the cold. He asked for me. Lou, in an extraordinary feat of memory, recognized him as Noah Hawksley, who had served with us in Poona as a mechanic. Inviting him in, but neglecting to offer him any refreshment, Lou quizzed Noah on life in Jamaica and told him that January was not a time to come to England

Happy times in Hackney

on holiday. Noah said that he was an immigrant, currently living in a dirty, cold hostel, and rapidly discovering that the streets of London were not paved with gold. Since I had told him to look me up if he was ever in England, he had come to find me and see if I could recommend a place to stay.

Lou, whose good heart often outweighed his deficiencies in the brain department, said that he could solve Noah's problem. Since he was moving out the next day, Noah could have his room. Noah, being a correct and God-fearing man, said he was sure that the room was not in Lou's gift, but Lou insisted and Noah, in dire straits, weakened.

Lou did not at first confess his offer when I came home from work. It was a convivial scene, with a uniformed Stanley at the kitchen table planning the traditional stag night pub crawl with Lou, much to my mother's disapproval. Offering Stanley a warm greeting, I asked if he had been driving anyone famous. Stanley said he had chauffeured the Air Minister, the Lord De Lisle and Dudley, which amused Lou greatly. He said that the name reminded him of a ventriloquist and his talking dog: 'What you been doing today, Dudley?' 'Well, your Lordship, I went up the Air Ministry and did a widdle on the carpet!' My mother, with her endearing if annoying sense of reverence towards those she saw as her betters, attacked Lou for speaking ill of a peer of the realm. Lou said that he was talking about a peer on the carpet. Stanley wondered if it was too late to talk Maggie out of her marriage plans. Such was the family banter and bonhomie which armed me for the bitter political struggles I had constantly to wage.

As I was changing into attire more suitable for a night on the town, Lou came to my room. In his typical roundabout manner, he managed to tell me about Noah's visit and, with rather less confidence, that he had offered Noah accommodation. Throughout my life, the colour of a man's skin has been immaterial – black, brown or coffee-coloured, we are all brothers, or sisters as the case might be. My mother was another matter. If at that time a black man had come to the door and said he had known me in the forces, she would certainly have asked him in and offered him a cup of tea, although she was likely to throw the cup away after he left. My principles were clear and unequivocal: if an old comrade was in trouble, he must be helped. I would do all in my power to achieve an equitable solution to the problem. Difficulties exist to be confronted. Thus I advised Lou that it was his responsibility to break the news to my mother and, in a halting way, he tried to, but his circumlocutions were such that she departed for Rita's house with her tray of sausage rolls, none the wiser.

We debated the matter in a pub. Stanley's argument was that, since Noah already knew Lou, he would not be surprised if I told him that Lou was barking up the wrong tree, and was not to be trusted. Lou registered some alarm at this, since Stanley was his best man, and references to untrustworthiness in his speech would not be well received. Stanley said he would present Lou in the best possible light. Declaring that the ties of wartime brotherhood were sacrosanct, and that I would naturally stand by him, I suggested telling Noah that the room had already been promised to Stanley. Stanley refused to be the scapegoat, pointing out that I had always brought him up to believe that right was right. I naturally agreed, in principle.

Our debate was interrupted by the arrival of Noah himself, full of gratitude for my offer of accommodation. What could I do but buy him a large rum and express my pleasure at the fact that he was coming to live with us?

Maggie rightly looks dubious as Rita lays down the law

As our convivial group settled down to toast Lou and Margaret's nuptials, a passing drunk ruffled Noah's hair, and called him Golly. Noah expressed his disapproval, while I pointed out that he and I had fought together for King and Empire. The drunk said that everyone knew I had been a clerk, which caused some entirely unnecessary laughter. Emboldened by this, the drunk compared negroes to cockroaches, and was about to utter some even more offensive insults when Stanley, demonstrating an ability of which I had hitherto been unaware, nutted him.

Some hours later, the triumphant stags made their way home singing, although our musical efforts tailed off into whispers as we approached the maisonette. Taking command as ever, I deployed my troops for the night; Stanley would sleep on the sofa, Noah in the bath. Stanley exhorted me to stand up to my mother, and we were discussing the matter when my mother herself appeared in the front door, calling us to order. As we sheepishly filed inside, I prepared myself to break the news about Noah. My mother, however, took him for the lucky chimney sweep, offering him a glass of sherry. The moment of reckoning was postponed.

While we men had been enjoying our carouse, a more ladylike event had been taking place *chez* Rita, although the tensions which Margaret's friend Veronica lent to any occasion were not far from the surface. Rita and Margaret disagreed about the length of the wedding dress, Rita wanting it longer, Margaret shorter since, as she

I keep this one of me and Mum in a frame by my bed

pointed out, she did not want to fall over. Veronica said that she had fallen over, and she was only wearing a day dress. Neither Margaret nor Rita wanted to pursue this unfruitful topic; Veronica's tales could be as Byzantine as Lou's. Rita said that longer was better, since a higher hemline made Margaret's feet look big. Margaret pointed out indignantly that Lou had measured them on his X-ray machine and pronounced them perfect.

Changing her line of attack, Rita said she felt a wedding dress was incomplete without a train; again Margaret disagreed. Veronica took Margaret's side. Trains were all well and good for going on honeymoon, she declared, but it was nicer to arrive at the church in a car. She and Ian had been to Bognor by train on their honeymoon, and Ian had obtained some rare engine numbers.

My mother's arrival at the party led Veronica to wax ever more lyrical on the pleasures of married life. Ian was saving up for a car, and would teach her to drive. They had a lovely little house in Welwyn Garden City, with a pond which Ian had dug. Increasingly irritated, Margaret pointed out that she also had a pond. But, said Veronica, it was Rita's pond. Rita, entering into the spirit of things, said that Veronica's pond was not hers, but belonged to Welwyn Garden City Borough Council. Veronica was not to be moved – it was their pond, containing their goldfish, and if they moved they would take the pond with them.

In a bucket, asked Rita? Pickfords would know what to do, Veronica replied. In any case, she and Ian would not move unless they had another baby. Was Margaret planning to have a baby? Margaret, understandably enraged, stormed from the room. Rita, congratulating Veronica on being a tower of strength, followed her. Oblivious, Veronica said that Ian also thought she was a tower of strength.

"I know you don't mean ill, Veronica," my mother said, "but it's not very thoughtful you going on about your house and your car and your babies, when all Maggie and Lou have got to start married life in is the spare bedroom and just three lungs between them. On top of which, Rita doesn't really want them under her roof." Veronica asked if that meant they were going to live in the loft. My mother, despairing, offered her another gin. Veronica declined; if she had any more than three, she would get silly.

Rita, meanwhile, was comforting Margaret, and musing aloud that it was a shame Lou and Veronica never fancied each other. Margaret sprang to her fiancé's defence, proclaiming him to be loving, faithful and cuddly. Rita pointed out that all these qualities were also available in dogs and, not for the first time, told Margaret that she did not have to go through with the wedding. Distraught, Margaret fled to her room. My mother came to investigate the commotion, and Rita explained that she had reminded Margaret of the old saying, 'marry in haste, repent at leisure', although her daughter had refused to listen. 'Strange,' said my mother, 'Harvey wouldn't listen when I said all that to him about you!' It was a conversation that my mother enjoyed recalling in her later years, invariably bringing a smile to her face.

The morning of the wedding dawned with the household peacefully slumbering.

Margaret proclaimed Lou to be loving, faithful and cuddly. Rita pointed out that all these qualities were also available in dogs

We suffered a rude awakening at 6.30, with a thunderous hammering on the door. Both my mother and I staggered downstairs; I reached the door first, haranguing the person on the other side, then modifying my outrage when I saw a policeman. He said he was looking for Stanley, immediately making my mother fear that we had been up to no good the night before. The policeman, youthful but self-important, said he could only divulge the nature of his mission to Stanley himself. It sounded a matter of the gravest importance, and it was with a sense of foreboding that I shook Stanley awake; he had managed to sleep through the entire kerfuffle. There was at first a sense of anti-climax when the policeman revealed that another driver had broken his leg, and Stanley was required to report immediately to Stanmore. My mother, a formidable sight in dressing-gown and curlers, accused the policeman of behaving like the Gestapo; then, recognizing him as 'little Ronnie Peacock', threatened to report him to his mother. This had a sudden deflating effect, and little Ronnie beat a strategic retreat. Lou, as ever, arrived late on the scene, and was stunned by the news that he had lost his best man. In response to Stanley's question as to whether he had other friends, Lou was unable to supply a name.

I am a man who invariably calls a spade a spade. Equally, I am a man who hates to cause distress

Stanley accelerated his dressing as a scream came from upstairs; my mother had gone to the bathroom and discovered Noah. Almost incoherent, she looked at me accusingly; did I know that the chimney-sweep was sooty all over? I explained that he was an old comrade from India, and that he was there at Lou's invitation. My mother demanded his immediate ejection and swept from the room, while I reminded Noah and Lou that this was my house, not hers. Lou wondered whether I would therefore ask my mother to leave, a question not worth the dignity of a reply.

At Rita's house, the tensions of the night before were still simmering. Veronica was engaged in a protracted telephone conversation with Ian, much to Rita's irritation, since the call was costing sixpence a minute. The fascinating minutiae of Veronica's domestic life were revealed in all their glory – her daughter had poured her drink all over Ian's mother's cat, and her son had thrown his breakfast all over the wall. Losing patience, Rita snatched the telephone from Veronica's hand, and bade Ian farewell. Ian was apparently unable to attend the wedding, since he had to work. At the time, he was engaged in the quality control of Shredded Wheat; Veronica stated that he had to taste every one, but that this was classified information, since spies from Kellogg's were everywhere. Or was it every thousandth Shredded Wheat that he had to taste? Margaret said that she thought Ian was allergic to milk. Veronica, pityingly, said that he washed them down with Tizer. Margaret, recounting these events in tranquillity, said that at least Veronica had distracted her attention from the rigours of the day to come.

The groom, meanwhile, was himself making a telephone call, having remembered that he indeed had a friend, a fellow patient in the Aberdeen sanatorium. Lou worked around gradually to the purpose of the call, first inviting his friend to the wedding, then asking if he would be best man. The friend acceded to both requests. Unfortunately, when Lou told him that the wedding was taking place that very afternoon, his friend

Opposite: *My old friend and comrade Noah Hawksley*

hung up. Lou told me that he was desperate. I told him that he was bonkers.

Noah, who was still with us, was reading job advertisements in the Hackney Gazette, and had found a likely prospect, a firm wanting an office manager cognisant with shipping and import–export documentation. Lou asked what cognisant meant. Noah explained that it meant having to know about something. Lou said that he did not know that. As kindly as I could, I explained to Noah that he was perhaps setting his sights too high in the racist conditions which pertained in 1953. Noah argued passionately that he should not lower his expectations because of his colour, and I was forced to agree.

It was at this point that my mother returned from the market, creating an immediate atmosphere of tension. Noah offered to leave, since he did not want to break up the happy home. My mother denied that the home was happy, saying that she did not expect to have to go through such things at her time of life. Noah immediately stood to leave, and I offered him my old greatcoat as protection against the weather. My mother muttered that I would not see the coat again. Noah, justifiably incensed, threw down the coat and stalked out. I told my mother that she should be ashamed, and she immediately agreed, mumbling that it was not Noah's fault he was coloured. Nevertheless, she did not wish to share her bathroom or kitchen with a black man. In a rare display of spirit I informed her that I had invited Noah to stay until he found somewhere of his own to live. My mother interpreted this as an eviction notice.

Brightly dawned their wedding day

Into this moment of high drama came a colleague from the council, Avis Pearson, a woman with whom I had been enjoying rather more than a strictly professional relationship. Although the flames had cooled on my side, they still burned bright on hers. As the reader may have gathered, I am a man who invariably calls a spade a spade. Equally, I am a man who hates to cause distress. Thus, rather than telling Avis that I did not wish her to accompany me to the wedding, I had let her down lightly by saying that Rita did not wish her to attend. My harmless deception had rather backfired, since Avis had bought a hat for the occasion, and in an emotional state had visited Rita the night before to display it, as she told me with some force. Avis suggested that I should have had the decency to tell her I no longer wished to pursue the relationship. Lou, unhelpfully, agreed with her. My mother, equally unhelpfully and entirely unjustifiably, suggested that I was a coward. Avis, thankfully, did not wish to debate the matter, instead presenting me with a petition designed to prevent the hanging of Derek Bentley.[17]

Veronica, Mags and Mum. I took this one!

She thrust it into my hands and, saying that she intended to see if Marshall and Snelgrove would take back the hat, left.

Lou had been thinking throughout this exchange, for him always a troublesome occupation; his furrowed brow suddenly cleared. Why, he suggested, did I not serve as his best man? I could escort Margaret into the church then, at the crucial moment, dodge around behind her and hand him the ring! I dismissed the idea out of hand, but said I had one of my own. Before I could explain it, there was a ring on the bell; a shivering Noah stood on the doorstep, having returned to borrow the coat. Lou had found his best man.

Life is a funny thing, as I often remark

It was time for me to be off. Wearing my new suit, I made my way to Rita's, where I found a radiant Margaret and a harassed Rita. As I was congratulating my beautiful daughter, Veronica asked what I thought of her appearance. I searched my mind for a suitable adjective; contenting myself with a compliment on how lime green suited her. Veronica preened. Gingerly, I broke the news about Stanley. Rita, typically, lost her temper and, equally typically, blamed me for the débâcle. 'I thought you'd changed, Harvey, I thought you'd got smarter,' she said. 'But you're still the berk I married!' I pointed out, entirely reasonably, that one could not argue with military law, and that I had managed to find a colourful

17. Derek Bentley, then nineteen, and Christopher Craig, aged sixteen and a half, were tried in 1952 for the murder of a policeman. Craig was saved from hanging because of his age, although he was the acknowledged ringleader and fired the shot after Bentley was already in custody. In spite of this, and in spite of a recommendation of mercy by the jury, Bentley was hanged later in the year, to an entirely justified public outcry. While I am all in favour of a good birching, capital punishment is quite another matter.

replacement. Rita was deflated, and I took advantage of the pause to produce my Derek Bentley petition but, as ever on these family occasions, the conversation became acrimonious. I suggested that Lou might well have found himself in a similar situation to Bentley, which upset Margaret. Veronica agreed with me, pointing out (perhaps redundantly) that Lou was not very quick on the uptake. Margaret said it had taken Veronica until she was thirteen to do joined-up writing. Veronica said it was because of her eye; Rita suggested that her brain might have something to do with it. Veronica took umbrage, declaring that Margaret could find another matron of honour. Rita said she was sorry to have described Veronica as stupid; the next time she would pretend that Veronica was clever. Peace restored, we set off for the church, squeezing ourselves into a rather inadequate Morris Eight.

It was a grey, drizzly day, but the weather did not dampen our spirits. As I stood on the threshold of the church, my little girl's hand clutching my arm, I gave Margaret a final opportunity to back out, an opportunity which she naturally refused. Veronica, in charge of the dress, fiddled around to such an extent that Margaret lost patience, twitching the skirt forward and precipitating Veronica into an undignified heap on the floor. The organist struck up the anthem, and we made our way down the aisle. I could not help but notice that, while the Moon side of the church was well populated, Lou occupied the other with only Noah for company. Poor Lou!

The service itself passed for me in a dream. My mind was filled with memories of Margaret throughout her life: the little blonde child squealing at a funfair; crying when she grazed her knee and running to daddy for comfort; uncomprehending but loyal at the Orient reserves, urging her heroic father on to yet greater deeds. I regretted the lost years of the war, for when I returned she was a young woman, a princess who could have married anyone she chose, a footballer, a film star ... instead she was marrying Lou Lewis. Life is a funny thing, as I often remark.

I could tell that the audience was in the palm of my hand, hanging on my words, applauding my sallies, wiping away an occasional tear

Afterwards, we gathered on the steps for photographs, marshalled by a rather aggressive young man. My mother refused his instructions to stand next to Noah, instead planting herself firmly beside me. I am ashamed to report that she said she could not show the photographs to friends if they included a darkie. Rita suggested that she show them the negatives instead. Noah offered to leave the group, but I would not hear of it. We were just about settled to the photographer's satisfaction when there was another interruption. A smart Humber drew up, and out jumped Stanley in his uniform, accompanied by an officer. Rita immediately, and typically, made a beeline for him, demanding to be introduced. Stanley said he was Squadron Leader Cunningham. Rita's eyes locked into his, a distasteful sight, but one with which I was sadly familiar. Margaret, too, had noticed her mother becoming flirtatious, a quite unbecoming sight for a woman of her age. Stanley took Noah's place in the wedding group, and harmony was restored.

At the reception, I busied myself with the petition. As I circulated among the guests, many of whom gratifyingly referred to me as Councillor Moon, I noticed that Veronica

Opposite: Maggie finally gets her man

had cornered Noah and was entertaining him with her inimitable conversation. I approached, to hear her confessing that she was now unable to listen to one of her favourite radio programmes, *Music While You Work*, since she did not work. Instead she was confined to *Housewives' Choice*. Noah appeared bemused. I took the opportunity to apologize to him for the quality of the music, since he had been a major attraction in the RAF dance band as a trumpeter. He played, as they say, a mean horn.

Then came the speeches. Stanley had thought his would not be needed, and had thrown it away. Noah offered his, which my mother snatched from his hand and gave to Stanley. Since it began by saying that Noah had known Lou since meeting in India in 1940, it was obviously inappropriate. My mother demanded to know how it continued.

"In the few short days since leaving an immigrants' hostel, I have been accepted into the Moon family with true Christian charity," Noah intoned. My mother looked uncomfortable. He winked at me when she was not looking.

In the event, Stanley improvised a few short words, heartfelt of course, but not quite comparable with my own remarks, which had been typed for me by my secretary. I had reassured her that ten pages of single-spaced typescript would not be over-long, and such was the case. Despite jocular cries of "Get on with it, Harvey", I could tell that the audience was in the palm of my hand, hanging on my words, applauding my sallies, wiping away an occasional tear. Rita, naturally, talked throughout to the Squadron Leader while my mother, overcome by her early start to the day, yawned copiously. Veronica rustled her way through my petition.

Opposite: *The dreaded Veronica*

Rita gets her claws into Tim Cunningham. She always did have an eye for a uniform

Then, all too soon, it was time for the young couple to embark on their epic voyage, two sailors setting off in their frail barque on the turbulent seas of married life. We gathered outside the church hall to wish them *bon voyage*. The photographer suggested that Margaret and Lou should run towards their car. Lou demurred, saying that he only had one and a half ... The photographer said that should not affect his running.

As they posed by the Morris, the Squadron Leader declared that they deserved rather smarter transport, ordering Stanley to drive them to the station in the Humber. When Stanley questioned the order, the Squadron Leader said that he would decide when they were due back at base. Then, taking Rita's hand, he whisked her back inside, leaving me with a familiar feeling of betrayal. A tearful Veronica began to hurl confetti after the car, at first multicoloured, then white. It took me some moments to realize that she was tearing up my petition.

CHAPTER FOUR

A LONG TIME IN POLITICS

AS MY OLD FRIEND HAROLD[18] remarked, a week is a long time in politics. Indeed, two weeks is a long time, three weeks is a longer time, and forty nine years is a very long time indeed. The fact that I would face the heat and burden of the day without a sight of evening was unknown to me as I entered Hackney Town Hall for my first council meeting. How innocent I was, how lacking in guile! A new boy, I recognized that my part was to keep my mouth shut, vote with my colleagues, and learn the ropes. I fear, however, that nature did not equip me with the capacity to blush unseen, and thus I found myself more often on my feet in Party meetings, and in full council, than was perhaps seemly. In a hothouse world where jealousy thrives, I could not but be aware of the whispers which followed me. I was accused, entirely unjustly, of seeking to curry favour, of jumping on bandwagons, even of seeking advancement! Those with whom I have worked over the years will know that advancement has been the last of my considerations. With Lord Moon (or Harvey Moon as I then was), the cause is all!

In those first, heady days, every cause demanded my selfless attention, but none was more urgent than housing. My voice was ceaselessly raised in the cause of the homeless, among whom I numbered myself after the explosion of the unexploded bomb and the destruction of Ladysmith Dwellings. I was proud to share the plight of so many in Hackney, content with my lot in an insalubrious, lice-ridden doss house.

Opposite: The happy couple prepare for married life

---

18. Harold Wilson, later Sir Harold Wilson, later Baron Wilson of Rievaulx, now sadly no longer with us.

My old landlord
Erich Gottleib has
an unwelcome
visit in his bakery
from an
environmental
health officer. His
sister Frieda took
the picture

What did it matter that I, effectively a single man, suffered privation when there were families with children, elderly people, the halt and the blind in an equal predicament?

I was about to leave the ward office one night, my secretary already having gone, when the telephone rang. A woman with a foreign accent said she had a flat to let in Stamford Hill, and did I know of a deserving family that could make use of it? My mind dwelt on the queue of desperate constituents who nightly came to seek my aid. Which of them could I recommend? The choice was invidious, but a choice had to be made. I told the woman that I would be sending a Harvey Moon to see her, and made my way to the house with the greatest possible speed.

My new landlord was called Erich Gottlieb, who shared the downstairs apartments with his sister, Frieda, who had made the telephone call. They were Austrian Jews, who had escaped from the Nazis in the nick of time. Erich had a bakery, in which he worked at night, so it was Frieda who showed me the upstairs rooms which I immediately took, arguing to myself that I would be a better servant to Down's Ward with my own roof over my head. My mother returned from Northampton, full of complaints about the stairs and about having to share a bathroom two floors down, but I emphasized to her that beggars could not be choosers, while ignoring the jibes of those who suggested that feathering my nest was my main concern. Throughout my political life, I have risen above such pettiness, allowing my record to speak for itself.

As time went by, I found myself increasingly drawn to the intelligence and sensitivity of my landlady, Frieda. Erich, whom I saw rarely, was something of a cold fish who,

I felt, disapproved of me. Frieda, on the other hand, had a warmth and a strength that I found most appealing. I discovered that she had ambitions to be an artist, while supplementing the income from the bakery with fine tailoring. As has been the case with so many women, I believe she was attracted by the aura of power which I exuded, even in 1946, together with my unshakeable principles.

It was on a matter of principle that I resigned from Hartley and Son, since Hartley refused to allow me leave to attend a TUC conference in Brighton on the closed shop. As a man of increasing political influence, it was my duty to attend. Standing at the podium, facing the vast arena, I summoned up all my not inconsiderable passion, delivering a speech which was at once witty and profound, incisive and moving; it was, although I say so myself, an oratorical tour de force. When it finished there was, quite naturally, applause. Sadly, it came only from a cleaner, since the conference did not begin until the next day and I had crept into the hall unobserved. It was, nevertheless, a foretaste of things to come, since I had the honour to address Congress on several occasions, my speciality being to move votes of thanks.

As has so often been the case, Lady Luck came to the rescue in my hour of need, this time in the unlikely shape of a thin, bald man, Harriet's old left-wing lawyer friend Dick Elliott, with whom I was sharing a boarding-house room at the conference. Dick said that the legal practice of Balfour, Elliott and Gunn was seeking a clerk, and asked if I would be interested. I told him that I would, and so at the grand old age of forty I became a junior member of the old-established firm. The term culture-shock had not then been invented, but culture-shock was what I felt when I received my first pay packet in the form of a cheque. Not only did I not have a bank account; my wages were less than I had been earning from Hartley. In a rare moment of depression, I told my mother that I must be the oldest office boy in the land. "Count your blessings, Harvey," she sagely replied, words of comfort which I invariably offer to those in distress.

I believe she was attracted by the aura of power which I exuded, even in 1946, together with my unshakeable principles

It must be said that blessings appeared few at the time. Combining my Labour Party duties with legal night-classes left me with little energy, and the lack of sympathy from the senior partner, Mr Quentin Elliott (naturally a Tory), led to me being fined an hour's wages when I accidentally nodded off during a lunch-hour. However, the ever-present Frieda provided solace, although her taste in art was somewhat too modern for me. Frankly, I could not then and cannot now see the attraction in dots and squiggles, and even less in the preservation of a raw sheep in formaldehyde. I may not know much about art, but I know what I like, and that is a picture which looks like a picture, or a sculpture which looks like a sculpture. In point of fact, several reproductions in resin of classical figures stand in my garden, together with an amusing life-size copy of the statue depicting a little boy answering an urgent call of nature, which serves as both fountain and conversation piece.

As I grew to know her better, Frieda confessed that the rooms which my mother and I were occupying had been kept empty in case other members of the Gottlieb family managed to escape the Nazi terror. Sadly, it appeared that none had, until a letter arrived from Cyprus. Yossela, a fifteen-year-old cousin of Erich and Frieda, had been interned there and wished to come to Britain. Frieda, with the faith of the weak woman in the strong man, implored my aid. In turn, I sought the advice of Dick Elliott, who encouraged me to pursue the matter myself, authorizing me to approach the Home Office with the weight of Balfour, Elliott and Gunn behind me. This I did, with satisfactory results, in that young Yossela arrived in Stamford Hill. However, it appeared that he was in some way mentally damaged, since he refused to speak, stabbed Stanley's football with a knife when I attempted to provide him with a friend close to his own age, and destroyed a portrait which Frieda was painting of me as a Christmas present. Then he disappeared.

She was unwilling to recognize that I was a grown man with a man's needs and responsibilities

A search-party was instituted but, as we discovered, Yossela had been hiding in the cellar. When my mother went upstairs after answering a call of nature, she found him cuddling the baby she had been minding in an attempt to earn a few pence and supplement my meagre income. The baby appeared to unlock something in his disturbed mind, and from being mute he was transformed into a young man who could not stop talking. It appeared that he wished to go to Israel to join other young Jews and, with the help of Margaret's friend Tom, he was smuggled on to a boat belonging to the company for which Tom worked.

My pivotal role in these events was recognized by Frieda with an increased degree of warmth, although she was under considerable pressure from her brother to take up with a man of her own persuasion. I can now confess that I occasionally spent the night in her arms, tiptoeing downstairs with an alarm clock when my mother was asleep, and tiptoeing back up before she awoke. Such are the subterfuges in which we take refuge when struck by Cupid's fatal dart! Our relationship was such that we began to discuss placing it on a more formal footing.

My mother, with a mother's instincts, was aware of developments, although, typically for a mother, she was unwilling to recognize that I was a grown man with a man's needs and responsibilities. She warned Frieda that I did not recognize the effect that I had on women. Frieda replied that she thought me very caring and very deep – she was a woman of great psychological insight.

My involvement with Frieda increased my understanding of the fears felt by Jewish people, and I was accordingly distressed when my mother returned from the market with a leaflet issued by the Union Movement which was not Socialist as the name suggests but was rather an organization espousing the doctrines of Fascism. My mother, never politically sophisticated, had been persuaded by their argument that British jobs should be for the British, and that races should not mix. In a few pithy phrases I corrected her thinking, and immediately set about organizing a rally to counter the Fascist threat to my beloved Hackney, an entirely disinterested move that had nothing to do with increasing Frieda's regard for me, nor with advancing my political career. Such things are above personal and political considerations.

Opposite: a pensive Frieda. Our relationship was colourful, to say the least

The meeting was, regrettably, thinly attended, although Rita's inamorato, Monty Fish, was notably present. Afterwards, Monty told me that two of the audience had

been members of the Union Movement, and that he was prepared to organize an assault on the Blackshirt menace. I said that I was only interested in non-violent action. He said he was only interested in bottling the bastards.

Meanwhile, my relationship with Frieda was under threat from Erich's disapproval. He refused to display my anti-Fascist leaflets in the synagogue, and said it was only out of respect for my mother that he had not evicted me from the house. I immediately offered to convert to Judaism if that would remove the obstacle to my marrying Frieda. Frieda said that she did not wish to be taken for granted. Women!

There was, of course, another obstacle to my marriage, namely the fact that I was still married to Rita. I took the opportunity to raise the matter with her during an outing to a greyhound racing event, but our discussion was inconclusive, since while I was engaged in a natural pursuit in the gentleman's conveniences I was the victim of a cowardly attack by a gang of Fascists! Had I not been attending to the matter in hand, I would have seen them off without difficulty. As it was, they took advantage of my preoccupation, then took to their heels.

I have always believed that a marriage prospers if the wife has a hobby

Frieda argued that I should inform the police, but I declared that I would deal with the matter in my own way, reluctantly involving Monty Fish in my plan. The following day I went to the market, making sure that the Fascists registered my presence. Then I ran towards a neighbouring warehouse, where it had been agreed that Monty and some of his young Jewish friends would be waiting in ambush, the Fascist bully-boys in hot pursuit. I was not dismayed, having taken the precaution of alerting the police, although I had not told Monty that. What was more dismaying, as I panted up the stairs, the boots of the Fascists ever closer behind me, was that there was no sign of Monty. Dodging behind a pillar, I spied a heaven-sent laundry basket, and leapt inside. From my hiding place I could hear the Fascists speculating as to my whereabouts, followed by the war-cries of Monty and his men. Raising the lid slightly, I could see that the good guys were in the ascendant. Then, as the sound of police whistles rang through the building, I lowered the lid, making sure that absolute silence had fallen before I climbed out and returned home in triumph.

Since Monty had solved my problem, I felt the least I could do was stand bail for him, although he had no intention of surrendering to it, planning instead to take refuge again in the Channel Islands. As he reimbursed me, I suggested that he might do me one more service, and took him to meet Erich. Always a colourful character, Monty laid it on thick, slapping Erich on the back, telling off-colour jokes, pressing cigars upon him, and congratulating him on his lovely daughter. Frieda, entering into the spirit of the occasion, told Erich that Monty would be escorting her to the synagogue's annual dinner and dance. As a result, Erich said he would be honoured if I would consent to be Frieda's escort.

So our relationship progressed, but as we grew closer the path grew bumpier. An early feminist, I assured Frieda that she could continue to paint after we were married, since I have always believed that a marriage prospers if the wife has a hobby. To my surprise, Frieda took umbrage, informing me that her art was a vocation rather than a pastime. In other ways, too, she asserted a degree of independence which I found hard to take, convinced as I am that a woman's place is in the home, nurturing and supporting the male breadwinner. In the end we agreed to differ, and Frieda left England for Paris where she could follow her Bohemian inclinations in the company of 'artistic' friends whose pretensions I frankly found insufferable, as I found their works incomprehensible. Since Erich had died she could afford to support herself; although I could never allow a woman to subsidize me, in her case I was prepared to make an exception.

Before she left, however, she was involved in the first political scandal to which my name was linked and in which, like the other scandals, I was entirely innocent.[19] Engaged in an artistic documentation of the people of Hackney, she was in my office sketching constituents when a clergyman arrived, saying that he had found a ration book and wished me to return it to its owner. I tried to explain that such was not a councillor's responsibility, but he disappeared, claiming to have a service to conduct. I placed the ration book in my desk drawer, locked it, and thought nothing more of the matter, until to my surprise Reg Baldock, one of my Tory opponents, accused me at the next Council meeting of being engaged in a "ration book

Councillor Moon makes a public appearance

fiddle". In my usual calm and measured way I invited him to step outside. As they say in parliamentary reports – uproar!

These baseless accusations, reported in the scurrilous local newspaper, the *Hackney Gazette*, perplexed me. I was further perplexed to be greeted by Stanley on my return home from work one night and told that two policemen were awaiting me upstairs. The policemen said that twenty stolen ration books had been found in the filing cabinet in my office, and would I care to comment? I told them that the office had been burgled, but that nothing had been stolen. It was obvious that the books had been planted in a crude attempt to intimidate me, but why? Recalling the mysterious vicar who had begun this affair, I invited Frieda to join us, and to show the policemen her sketch. They immediately identified him as 'Dead Body Wilson', a well-known Fascist associate, but their suspicions remained unallayed.

Never a man to sit back in a crisis, I went to visit Reg Baldock, and in my usual reasonable way suggested that if he did not tell me what was going on, and what had prompted his scurrilous accusations, I would inform his wife about the affair he had been carrying on with a young woman called Linda Rice. Neither Reg nor Linda was particularly discreet, and it was surprising that his wife was not aware of the

---

19. For a detailed refutation of these 'smear' attempts, see Chapter 5 of *The Moon Memoirs*, Volume 1, op. cit.

situation, since it was common knowledge among councillors of all persuasions. Reg said that not only was he carrying on with Linda; there had been another girl during the war. The Fascists had learned about both, and had used their knowledge to force Reg into his campaign of vilification against me. So I was too late with my attempt at blackmail. Telling Reg that the word 'blackmail' was foreign to my vocabulary, and that I was engaged only in friendly persuasion, I retired to consider my strategy. If Reg could not be persuaded, then something else had to be done, although for the life of me I could not think what. Meanwhile, I was irritated to find that my every step was being dogged by a representative of the *Gazette* who was taking an entirely unjustified interest in my private life. Not only had he sought to speak about me to Rita; he was also asking questions about Frieda.

It was at this time that I formed a philosophy of the Press that has guided me ever since. In my view, the Press exists to report what it is told. So-called investigative journalism serves only to debase the coinage of political life; a politician should be judged on his public persona, not on the minutiae of a private life which is of no interest to anyone but himself. Unless, of course, he is a Tory.

I was about to sit down to a convivial Christmas lunch when Baldock telephoned me. He was incoherent. Call it second sight, call it sensitivity, but something impelled me to make my way as speedily as I could to his house. There I found him with his head in an unlit gas oven. Dragging him away, I opened the doors and windows. Baldock confessed that the Fascists had told his wife about his infidelities, and that she had left him. He was pathetically grateful when I offered him my hand and, in the magnanimous spirit of Christmas, pronounced my forgiveness; who among us can say that they have not sinned? I waited until Boxing Day was over before telephoning the *Gazette*.

If the Baldock episode taught me anything, it was that the Press can wield considerable power. Hence, swallowing my scruples, I made it my business to befriend the Gazette reporter, one Fred Lawrence. He initiated me into the secrets of the inky trade; I ensured that he was made aware of the important issues that occupied our time on the Council. We met in a pub outside the borough in case anyone should draw misleading conclusions from seeing us together. Fred was a good listener, and was particularly interested in the titbits I was able to feed him about the personalities of the day. Although never one to gossip, I am afraid that, under the influence of his generous hospitality, I may have committed an occasional indiscretion. If I did, it was entirely without malice, and certainly with no sense of self-aggrandizement.

Fred was a helpful ally at a difficult time when my position came under threat, as a result of scurrilous tittle-tattle about my private life. A man of conscience, I invariably voted on issues as they arose, listening to discussion, weighing up the arguments, then lending my weight to the side that seemed to be in the ascendant. Neither right-wing nor left-wing, I have always been an independent man. As a result, I at times suffered the disfavour of one group or another among my colleagues, and in this instance it was the right-wing that was seeking to discredit me by spreading falsehoods about

I read personally any book which carried the slightest trace of raciness or obscenity to ensure that it was fit for public consumption

Opposite: A candidate with high hopes

•77•

my private life. It was said that I was living with a bohemian artist while my wife was consorting with a supposed homosexual, and that I had paid a visit to the seaside with a prostitute in order to allow divorce proceedings to be instituted. Such pathetic scandal was beneath my contempt, even if the accusations were true.

As chairman of the libraries committee, a member of the housing committee, and a Justice of the Peace, I recognized that such scurrilousness had to be fought so that I could continue to serve the people of Hackney. Were I forced to resign, who knows what left-wing firebrand might take my place? Casting about for a means of fighting these dastardly whispers, I found an answer in my unwavering patriotism. At the time, the Russians were blockading Berlin, and an airlift had been launched by the Allies as a means of supplying the beleaguered city. What could I do but volunteer to lend my expertise to this new fight against oppression? I wrote immediately to the Air Ministry.

Avis informed me that if I continued to sit on the fence, I would end up with a spike in an unfortunate place

Taking my old RAF uniform from the wardrobe, I found that it still fitted me well, apart from a certain tightness in the trouser department. Frieda, with her nimble fingers, made the necessary adjustments. I then summoned Fred to the house, suggesting that he should bring a photographer, and announced that I was going to re-enlist. A personal summons to the Air Ministry was no more than I could expect, and I set off with high hopes and a certain sense of trepidation. Ushered into the presence of a typically languid brass-hat, I made my case. As a stores clerk with a distinguished record, my warehousing abilities should surely enable me to play a vital role in the airlift operation. I was fit, and ready to go wherever the Ministry wished to send me. The Wing Commander listened to me with close attention, congratulated me on my war record, but told me: not today, thank you. This was naturally distressing news, but my spirits were raised when the *Gazette* was published, carrying a large photograph of my uniformed self, together with a rather gratifying headline.[20] The immediate danger over, I still had to confront questions as to why I was still in Hackney. Saying that I was on the reserve provoked some thoughtless jibes about my pre-war status with Orient, but the immediate crisis passed, and the episode faded from people's minds. Frieda's departure and my consequent unhappiness meant that I did not pursue the matter of divorce, and there matters rested.

Meanwhile I threw myself heart and soul into politics, ensuring that books acquired for the borough's libraries were of a suitably improving nature, championing the cause of that fine flier Biggles over the somewhat insipid fare offered by Enid Blyton, and reading personally any book which carried the slightest trace of raciness or obscenity to ensure that it was fit for public consumption. Only the best was good enough for my people. The Naked and the Dead, for example, attracted my keen attention, although its title misled me somewhat.

I would discuss these issues long into the night with my colleague Councillor Avis

---

20. 'Hero Harvey to Fight Red Menace: Moon to Challenge Might of Moscow'. Given the sensational demands of newspapers, this seemed to me to be justifiable hyperbole, although I naturally remonstrated with Fred, who appeared erroneously to believe that these were the words I myself had dictated. The scope for misunderstanding with journalists is truly vast!

Pearson, and so keen was the ideological debate that I frequently found I had missed the last bus. My way with words, and my frequent insights which cut to the heart of the matter, served only to fan the flames. Her way with cocoa was unparalleled in my experience. Avis, however, stood further to the left than I, and in time I wearied of her certainties, as well as her insistence on carrying the debate forward into the early hours. After all, a man needs his sleep. It was unfortunate that our relationship should have come to an end at the time of Margaret's wedding, but in every joy there is sorrow.

Avis, together with the ward secretary Gordon Hopkins, was mentor to a new breed of party activist, the post-war generation, who claimed with the arrogance of youth that many in the old guard had run out of ideas and were lacking in radicalism. Their watch-cry was 'democratic socialism', and they argued that long-serving councillors wished only to keep down the rates and lead a quiet life. The young hotheads also claimed that the 'ruling clique', as they referred to those in power, was too friendly with the Conservative opposition. As ever, I was torn between both points of view. In one sense, I was part of the post-war generation myself. In another, I was not, being older and having come to politics later in life. My attempts to be judicious were not always greeted with the respect they deserved; in a heated moment, Avis informed me that if I continued to sit on the fence, I would end up with a spike in an unfortunate place.

Such an accusation was grossly unfair, since I have always been a firm believer in several causes at a time.

A postcard from the honeymooning couple

Welcome to MARGATE

For example, my service in India (despite my unfortunate experience with the Gurkhas) left me with the insight that all are equal under the skin. I had no truck then, and have none now, for discrimination on the basis of colour. Even before the arrival of my old

Discussing the plight of black immigrants was one thing; having one living in my house was quite another

comrade Noah Hawksley, who had unknowingly helped to shape my beliefs, I was seized with a desire to ensure a welcome for our negro brethren, who were already coming to 'the mother country' in increasing numbers. I took an opportunity to raise the matter in the housing committee, suggesting that Hackney should be prepared to play its part in providing homes for immigrants. The committee chairman and our leader, Councillor Conroy, made light of my suggestion in insulting terms, drawing the meeting to an abrupt close since, typically, he wished to adjourn to the Anchor where he said there was a pint with his name on it.

Discussing the plight of black immigrants in the abstract was one thing; having one living in my house was quite another, particularly since my mother's unrelenting hostility was extremely wearing on the nerves. Coming down to breakfast one morning, my mother informed me that Noah had already gone to the Labour Exchange in search of work. Since it was only seven thirty, I was surprised. My mother said she had suggested that Noah get there early. Again I read the riot act, asking how long my mother intended to maintain her hostility. She replied that it depended on how long Noah was staying. In any case, she found his presence uncomfortable, since one heard so many things about black men and white women. She drew her dressing gown around her as she spoke. I wondered aloud whether the sight of my mother in her hairnet was driving Noah wild and, knowing a good exit line when I heard one, left.

He was quite naturally depressed on his return. Nearly every vacancy specified 'no coloureds', and the only job which he had been offered was that of lavatory attendant. Although he was desperate for work, Noah felt that an experienced office manager should not be asked to sink so low. A proud man, he confessed that he had run out of money, even to the extent of having pawned his trumpet. I said I had not known that he still played. Noah said that to play without a trumpet was impossible. More seriously, he asked for my help in finding employment, a request to which I could not but accede, in the meantime offering him a ten shilling note and assuring him that all of my not inconsiderable energy and influence would be devoted to his cause. My mother interjected that my influence had been unable to obtain a house, something on which she had set her heart, but I chose to ignore her. Sometimes, despite my devotion, I found my mother intensely irritating (sorry, Duchess!).

That night Hopkins was in attendance at one of our regular ward meetings, which were increasingly attended by new faces, all of a left-wing persuasion. One of them, by the name of Robinson, stood up and read out a question which he and Hopkins had obviously prearranged; Hopkins's crabby handwriting was easily recognizable. The

My mother sometimes found Noah's playing hard to take. Rita had no such problems

question was addressed to me. In Councillor Conroy's absence, did I have anything to say about rumours of corruption over the award of Council building contracts to a member of the Tory opposition? I replied that they were not rumours, but more scurrilous attacks on the reputation of our Council leader. Then why, asked Hopkins, was Conroy having dinner at the home of that same Tory councillor this very night? This outrageous slur provoked uproar. Adopting my traditional role as peacemaker, I suggested that this was neither the time nor the place for such issues to be addressed. Hopkins, mistaking my meaning, accused me of wishing the matter to be swept under the carpet, adding that the voters of Down's Ward deserved representatives who were not afraid to practise their Socialist principles. I offered to give him a thick lip. Avis hurriedly closed the meeting. I hung behind to talk to her, suggesting that if she heard I was to be a left-wing target, then I would be grateful to know. Avis was cool. Setting personal interests aside, I pleaded Noah's cause, and she said she would do her best on his behalf, rejecting my offer of a drink for old time's sake with a terse 'Get lost!'. Men are so much more logical when it comes to affairs of the heart.

Returning home with what I hoped was encouraging news for Noah, I found Lou and Margaret back from their honeymoon. They had thoughtfully bought us all presents that, as Lou pointed out, had 'A gift from Margate' written on them. Lou had bought me a pair of cufflinks, but one of the swivels was rather stiff. In an attempt to loosen it, he swallowed the cufflink. Ever philosophical, he offered to return it to me in a couple of days.

Noah asked if she thought he preferred to dance around a pot of boiling missionary with a bone through his nose

Soon afterwards my mother made another attempt to rid herself of Noah, suggesting that he should return home, since the climate and the lack of hostility would surely suit him better. Impassioned, Noah told her that he felt he belonged in Britain because, after all, he was British. When he was at school he had learned British history; all his life, he had been made to feel British. No one had queried his colour when he volunteered for the RAF. As far as he was concerned, he was staying! My mother, somewhat taken aback, congratulated him on his pluck. Then, making an unexpectedly magnanimous gesture, she went to her bedroom, returning with an old pair of long johns, which had belonged to my father. While Noah was deliberating on his response, Avis arrived. She had not been able to find a suitable job for him; the best vacancy she could find was for a road-sweeper. I began to remonstrate, but Noah stopped me. He would take it, he said.

The following weekend saw the climax of my mother's gradual reconciliation with our guest. As was her practice, she had gone to church, where the Vicar preached a stirring sermon about brotherhood. On her way out, she was surprised to find Noah beside her in the queue of parishioners waiting to shake the Vicar's hand. Noah asked if she thought he preferred to dance around a pot of boiling missionary with a bone through his nose. The Vicar shook her hand and wished her well. Ignoring Noah, he shook the hand of the woman behind him. My mother, to her eternal credit, took Noah's arm, reminded the Vicar of the sentiments which he had just expressed, and swept Noah away in triumph. After that, although we had our ups and downs, Noah was an honorary Moon.

Opposite: Noah Hawksley, the man with the golden horn!

While he did not confess it to us at the time, Noah was making plans. With his first week's wages, having paid for his keep, he bought an overcoat and shoes. At the end of the second week he made straight for the pawnbrokers to reclaim his trumpet. We did not realise how much he had missed it until the trumpet became an inescapable part of our lives, a very noticeable one in the confines of a maisonette, it must be said. Not only did he renew acquaintance with his instrument; Noah met a fellow musician engaged on the same errand. The musician, Carl Fantozzi, suggested that Noah should go to Archer Street in Soho on a Monday morning. It was an informal job-market for musicians, not dissimilar to the system employed in the docks. Noah registered the information.

In the meantime, he brought his trumpet home and played loudly and enthusiastically. It nearly made my mother declare him undesirable again. Rita, on a rare visit, found it extremely desirable, declaring in her typical fashion that he had nearly blown her out of her nylons. I resisted the riposte that they were easily removed. Noah's yearning to make music, coupled with the unseasonable weather which penetrated his blue serge uniform and the coat which he wore over it in defiance of regulations, made him determine to abandon the road sweeper's life. I offered to provide him with a reference to take to the Labour Exchange, suggesting that my considerable reputation, together with a smart appearance, should help him to obtain a white collar job. He responded that it was the black face above the white collar that was the problem.

She was Helen Lawrence, a singer I had enjoyed in Singapore who performed with the Kenny Rankin Orchestra

Once again unemployed and the object of my freely-given charity, Noah was excited to receive a telephone call from his pawnshop acquaintance, Carl Fantozzi. Carl had been asked to join a band at a jazz club in Soho, the Flamingo, and had suggested Noah as a possible trumpeter. I had not seen him so excited since Lou fell from an elephant in Poona. With his excitement went nerves, and he asked if I could accompany him to his audition. I was delighted to agree, particularly since I was not then a *habitué* of the cosmopolitan quarter.

We descended the stairs into the stuffy Soho basement, smelling in equal parts of stale perfume, cigarette smoke, sweat and liquor. Some may have found the mixture somewhat too rich for their appetites; I confess that I found it quite to my taste. Having made clear to Carl that I was Noah's friend rather than his manager, Noah went with him to meet the leader of the band, Syd, while I perched on a stool, savouring the atmosphere. I did not at first see a blonde woman who appeared behind the bar, and jumped when she spoke, informing me that the club did not open until seven. Having explained my identity, she became somewhat more friendly, regretting that she could not offer me a drink. I mistook her for the barmaid, an embarrassing error since later she told me she was the manageress. We introduced ourselves; her name was Helen Lawrence. It was a name that had a certain resonance, and I searched through the filing cards of my mind to explain it. Of course! She was the Helen Lawrence, a singer I had enjoyed in Singapore who performed with the Kenny Rankin Orchestra, and whom I had heard from time to time on the wireless. It transpired that she had been married to Kenny Rankin, had nursed him through his final illness, and was now

a widow, preferring to manage the club rather than to resume her career. I was strangely disappointed when she terminated the conversation and walked away.

Noah's audition was successful, and I decided to organize a family outing to support him. Since I thought Margaret and Lou would enjoy the occasion I had invited them, though I knew that the price for their attendance would be the company of Rita. Even my mother, who generally went to bed at nine o'clock, was determined to come, appearing in the coat which she had worn for my father's funeral. She declared that she did not want to be mistaken for one of Soho's more colourful female denizens, who smoked in the street and did not carry handbags. Her own was particularly capacious.

In the event, she rose to the occasion with the spirit so typical of her, tapping her feet surreptitiously to the music and indulging in more gin than was her wont. Rita, naturally, felt entirely at home. I was ordering drinks at the bar when I again met Helen Lawrence, who appeared gratifyingly pleased to see me. Ever the gentleman, I asked her to join me in a drink, which she declined, although she did consent to dance. In the course of the conversation, I happened to mention that Rita was my ex-wife, and that my children were grown-up. I do not generally offer personal information on first or even second acquaintance, but there was something sympathetic about Helen, something which made me feel that I could confide in her.

Much as I wished to dally, I thought that I should take my mother home before the gin had too deleterious an effect and, in any case, Helen had business to attend to. As we ascended the stairs, my mother staggering slightly, I felt that the Flamingo Club and I would not be strangers for long. We made our way towards Rita's car, and it was then that we encountered Stanley, red-faced under the red light. Happy days!

> *There was something sympathetic about Helen, something which made me feel that I could confide in her*

Opposite: *Moon the thinker*

CHAPTER FIVE

TEA FOR TWO

೪ఎ

WHILE COUNCIL MATTERS OCCUPIED LARGE AMOUNTS OF MY TIME, I was equally active in the legal sphere. This led to the frequent comment that people did not know how I managed to combine my various interests. My invariable response was to laugh modestly, before embarking on an explanation of how I organized my time. Perhaps, in retrospect, I offered a little too much detail, since it was rarely that anyone managed to hear me through. This was a pity, since I possessed a fund of anecdotes about both the libraries committee and about my occupancy of the Bench of Magistrates. A JP until I resigned on my election as MP for Burslem, I was unceasing in my commitment to the administration of justice, treating every case before me with the patience and understanding for which I became a byword.[21]

As I have already recounted, I was recruited to the firm of Balfour, Elliott and Gunn by Dick Elliott,[22] or Mr Dick as he was known in the practice as a means of differentiating him from his father, Mr Quentin. At first I was greeted with profound hostility. Mr Quentin, an arch-Tory, disapproved of my Labour Party activities, and of my friendship with his son. Geoffrey Rider, the senior clerk to whom I was then responsible, resented

---

21. To remove any possible misunderstanding, even at this distance in time, I once again deny that I was the Hackney magistrate "whose scandalous private life and cat-naps on the bench threatened to bring the court into disrepute", as the Evening News claimed in an ill-researched exposé (17 December 1950).

22. Richard Elliott (Baron Elliott of Spring Hill) 1900-1985. MP for mid-Beds. 1947-1982; Labour Whip, Shadow Minister of Trade, Junior Home Office Minister, Minister of Health, Spokesman on Overseas Development in the House of Lords.

Opposite: Helen Lawrence, a talented singer and a close friend

my friendship with Dick. They were difficult times, but my undoubted abilities, coupled with my innate charm, gradually broke down barriers.

When Rider suffered a nervous breakdown on the death of Mr Quentin, I became senior clerk in his stead, taking the burden of the practice on my shoulders, since Dick was by this time a Member of Parliament and devoted little time to the office. Under my careful tutelage the two junior clerks for whose appointment I had argued strongly, referring in dramatic terms to my onerous workload, undertook a great deal of the work, allowing me to exercise the supervisory functions for which I was so admirably fitted and for which I ensured I was adequately remunerated. Having two keen youngsters who owed me their jobs and their loyalty in the office, as well as a secretary of my own, I was able to take occasional leave of absence with an entirely clear conscience.

They were difficult times, but my undoubted abilities, coupled with my innate charm, gradually broke down barriers

I was paying some desultory attention to the Daily Telegraph (not, of course, a Socialist newspaper, but one which offered admirable coverage of the news and, indeed, an admirable crossword), puzzling over the answer to the clue 'Get very close to a very quiet fish', eight letters,[23] when I received an anguished telephone call from Lou Lewis. He was, as ever, somewhat incoherent, but the gist of it was that he had been falsely accused of defrauding Burgess's department store. I immediately made my way there, to be greeted by Lou's trusting smile. Whatever his problems, he had always relied on me to sort them out. Armstrong, the store detective who had apprehended Lou, and his superior, Cedric, asked if I was Lou's solicitor. I replied with only the slightest deviation from the truth that I was his legal adviser, and requested a private consultation with my client.

At first he prevaricated, but eventually the full story came out. It was a simple fiddle devised by Cedric, who might have been an adequate shoe salesman but did not figure highly in the ranks of master criminals. A customer would buy a pair of shoes and proffer the correct money, say, £2 10s (or £2.50 for my younger readers). Cedric would ring up £1 10s, pocket the difference, and then split the money with Lou. This explained the sudden rash of presents which Lou had been pressing on Margaret, but did not explain his stupidity in going along with a scheme which was bound to fail. The decline in takings from the shoe department had aroused the suspicions of the management, and a decoy customer had been used to obtain proof. The store detective confronted the malefactors. Cedric at first tried to bluster, claiming that he had made an honest mistake. Then he accused the store of playing a despicable trick. Lou, who suffered from a nervous bladder, made an attempt to go to the lavatory, but Armstrong had cornered his prey.

Lou, returning much relieved from the lavatory, told me that he was prepared to go to court and face the music, saying that he would plead extenuating circumstances, such as his wartime record and his damaged lung. Since this was a critical time in my political life I forbade him to do any such thing, and negotiated with Armstrong. If the

23. The answer, kindly supplied by Wendy, my secretary, was of course approach.

money was refunded, and Lou left immediately, would the store agree not to prosecute? After all, Lou was a hapless dupe, and Cedric was obviously the prime mover, taking advantage of a weak, albeit well-meaning man, a man not in the best of health, who had served with distinction in the RAF, whose domestic circumstances were such that ... Armstrong asked me to spare him the sob story, and invited me to remove Lou from the building before he changed his mind.

Cedric on the fiddle at Burgess's

As was only fair, I offered to loan Lou the money, although Rita, doing the right thing for once, said that she would pay half. Lou was extremely cast down by this chain of events, absent-mindedly smoking despite his lung, and telling Margaret that he was of no use to her. Margaret insisted that he snap out of it, although the lack of his wages would mean that the time when they could have their own house was ever more distant. Wishing to spare my mother distress, I told her that Lou had been laid off because of staff cutbacks, although Lou, incapable of discretion, blurted out the truth and had to suffer a prolonged lecture in return.

His unemployed state cast the family into gloom, not lightened by his extreme choosiness about what work he could do. The notorious lung featured ever more strongly, much to Rita's irritation. Indeed, the sight of Lou in his dressing gown drooping around the house, stealing her cigarettes and listening to the wireless, drove her to distraction. One morning she instructed him sharply to collect the laundry for the

Squadron Leader
Tim Cunningham

Happy Curl, lung or no lung, which provoked entirely unexpected consequences.

Encountering Noah at the Labour Exchange, Lou persuaded him to carry the laundry, and they arrived together at the salon to find Rita poring over her account books. Her accountant was away, and the books had to be completed. Noah offered to look at them for her, since he had dealt with accounts in the shipping office in Jamaica. So, while Lou listened to *Children's Hour*, Noah strove to make sense of Rita's creative approach to book-keeping. *Children's Hour* over, Lou came to see what progress Noah was making and, idly looking at totals, discovered that the Happy Curl was unexpectedly profitable. He kept the information to himself as Rita came home, surprised to find the curtains drawn. Noah said he had not wanted to be a cause of gossip among the neighbours. Rita flung back the curtains and made a speech. "I may be only lower middle class," she said, "I may not have had the advantages, but I have never been bourgeois. I don't give a monkey's toss what the neighbours think, if you'll pardon my French. They're petty people, and I've always felt a stranger in their midst!" Noah was impressed, but still demurred when she suggested going with him to a Greek café. Rita would have pursued the matter, but the telephone rang and the moment was lost, although as Rita helped Noah on with his coat she suggested that a drink in Soho would not be a cause of gossip.

Meanwhile, Lou had told Margaret what he had seen in the books, persuading

her that she was being taken advantage of. Margaret, incensed, confronted her
mother, who refused to discuss the matter. After some days of frost, Rita thought
she had found a solution. The average wage for a stylist was five guineas a week,
and she was paying Margaret £5 10s. On due consideration, she felt that she could
afford £6. Margaret thought that this was fair, since the cost of living was always
on the increase. Rita agreed. Because of the cost of living, she was raising Lou and
Margaret's rent by 7s 6d.

After that it was war. Margaret went looking for new jobs and achieved an interview
at Selfridge's, but she was turned down because of her accent – pure snobbery, in
my view. Had she been in a similar position in the 1960s, when gorblimeys
ruled smart society, there would have been no problem. Her next ploy
was to make appointments with regular clients in their homes, a tactic
that reduced Rita to gibbering rage. Having been a manageress rather
than a stylist, my former wife's attempts to fill the gap left by Margaret
were haphazard in the extreme. Something had to be done, particularly
since Margaret sought to involve me in the dispute as her councillor after
Rita's self-control had snapped and she had given Margaret a clip round
the ear. She stormed into my office demanding to know how she could
organize a strike. I could, of course, have advised her, but it was not a
dispute in which I wished to embroil myself. Hence I told Margaret frankly
and with all due consideration that both she and her mother represented
a pain in the nether regions, and that she should negotiate a compromise.
She did not warm to this advice.

I could, of course, have advised her, but it was not a dispute in which I wished to embroil myself

In the end, Rita's business sense prevailed, and she agreed that
Margaret should become a partner. Margaret immediately launched into
special offers, new styles and a reorganization of the salon, leaving Rita
with little to do but answer the telephone and think about men, although in the
latter she needed little encouragement. After her experience of Noah in full cry at the
Flamingo, she determined to set her cap at him. Meanwhile, Squadron Leader
Cunningham was setting his cap at her. Having arranged a date with Noah, she broke
it when Tim Cunningham arrived with a better offer: tickets to see Danny Kaye. Noah
was not unnaturally confused and angry, believing that Rita preferred a white man to
him. He took his courage in both hands and asked for my advice, something which
amused my mother greatly as she sat in her chair, pretending to be asleep. In the end,
chuckles overcame her at the idea of anyone asking my advice about Rita. I confess
that I did not find it as amusing as she did. Naturally I gave Noah my blessing, while
warning him about the essentially fickle nature of the woman with whom he was
dealing. I could say though, with entire honesty, that colour meant nothing to Rita;
the colour of a man's skin, the colour of his trousers ... on the trail, she was a lioness
seeking whom she might devour.

I was at the time doing some stalking myself. Having been strangely attracted by
Helen Lawrence, I took to dropping in at the Flamingo on my way home from work.
Soho was not actually on my way home at all, but I pretended that it was, although
Helen saw through the subterfuge immediately. The early evening was a marvellous

time, since I could have Helen more or less to myself, give or take the waiters setting out the tables, a musician or two practising, and possibly some Soho types muttering confidentially to one another in a dark corner. I took care not to show too much interest in them, since I have always had a high regard for my personal safety, and after a time they came to ignore me. I told my mother that I was working late in case she became suspicious, although why a man in his late forties should feel the need to lie to his mother is something I cannot adequately explain. Doubtless Dr Freud could help!

Helen chattered in her womanly way about this and that, while I was always eager to meet her requests for tales of legal life or Council doings. One night while my mother was in hospital, I took the opportunity to spend an evening at the Flamingo. Dancing with Helen, talking of inconsequential things, I could not fail to see that she was abstracted. I gave her an old-fashioned look. She asked me why I was pulling such a strange face. I explained that it was an old-fashioned look, which produced a smile. She told me her preoccupation was due to the return of a former boyfriend who, she explained, was not a very nice man. I was more concerned to establish how former

Helen tries to remove a speck of dust from my eye

was former; debating whether or not to give my heart to Helen, I had not envisaged competition. She reassured me. The man, Phil Azzopardi, was out of the picture, although he imagined he was still in the centre of the frame.

Shyly, Helen confessed that she had needed help in disentangling her late husband's affairs, and Azzopardi had been there in her hour of need. The fact that he was a gangster had not, at the time, appeared relevant. I asked why she had pursued the relationship if he was such an undesirable? She told me frankly that it had been a mistake. Azzopardi had just got back to London from a speedily-arranged cruise, while some furore with the law died down. Now he had returned, prepared to pick up the threads. Drawing myself up to my full five foot seven, I told her that she had nothing to fear. I was more than a match for some Maltese wide-boy, and I would tell him where to get off at the first available opportunity.

This came somewhat earlier than I had anticipated. One Saturday I was alone in my office at Balfour, Elliott and Gunn, with only the ever-faithful Wendy for company, when there was a knock at the door. Wendy went to see who our visitor was. She returned with the news that it was a Mr Azzopardi. At first the name meant nothing, then I realized who it was. With my usual resolution I instructed Wendy to ask him what he wanted. Then I told her to suggest that he should return after business hours. Or should he be asked to make an appointment? Tired of my dithering, Wendy showed him in. I offered him tea, the drink of a civilized Englishman. He looked as if he would have preferred some alcoholic beverage, but said that tea would be acceptable.

I asked Wendy to provide it, and began to make polite conversation but, with the lack of manners typical of his kind, Azzopardi interrupted me, telling me in the crudest terms of the services he had provided to Helen, financial as well as personal. I raised my hand to shut off the flow, but he continued, saying that he was there to introduce himself, and to make a suggestion. At this point, Wendy arrived with the tea tray. I asked him what suggestion he had in mind. He told me that I should remove myself. I suggested, reasonably, that Helen should decide the matter. In response, Azzopardi picked up the teapot and, offering to be mother, poured a stream of tea in my lap. As I writhed in agony, Azzopardi draped his coat over his shoulders and sauntered out, informing me that next time I could expect hard-boiled eggs. Fortunately there was no lasting damage, since my trousers were always rather Hammersmith Palais, as we used to say in my youth – that is, plenty of ballroom.

A cow pushed its nose through the window, nudging me intimately at a rather crucial moment

Helen was horrified when I told her how Azzopardi and I had shared tea for two, and insisted on making a minute inspection of the wounded area. I encouraged her to linger as long as she wished. Since she was then living with her mother, and I lived with mine, trysting places were rather difficult to find. The dressing-room at the Flamingo was more of a cupboard than a room, stank strongly of jazz musicians, and was always liable to interruption. An experiment in her car was something of a failure when a cow pushed its nose through the window, nudging me intimately at a rather crucial moment. In the event, we made do with my desk, which was practical, if not romantic.

As Helen and I were cementing our relationship, equally momentous things were happening in the rest of the family, not least to Lou. Visiting my mother one evening, he was much taken by the somewhat overpowering personality of our local tallyman,[24] Charley Ross. Charley, a frustrated music hall performer, erupted into the flat, rattled off some rather dubious jokes which nevertheless amused my mother, then spotted Noah, whom he characterized as a Robinson's Golly tootling on the trumpet. Noah was not amused, particularly when Charley launched into an Al Jolson routine. My mother called him to order and Charley, scenting the potential loss of a customer, became immediately contrite, offering my mother half a yard of knicker elastic and a card of pins as a bribe to regain her affections. However, on learning Noah's name, he could not resist asking if he had come over in a whale. Noah left the room.

Lou wondered if anyone could be a tallyman, provoking the retort from my mother that it was the ideal profession for anyone with long pockets and short arms. This sally was rather beyond Lou, who paused for a while to consider it. Charley asked whether Lou had ambitions in that direction. Ever cautious, Lou said that he had only one lung, which sent Charley into peals of laughter. "One-lung Lou?" he said. "You sound like a Chinaman!" When Lou said that he had been a salesman, and my mother added that he had been sacked for stealing, Charley looked at him with new respect, and invited him to take tea at the café round the corner, where he explained the mysteries of the tallyman's craft, and offered to sell Lou some stock to start him off. Lou felt that he had found his role in life.

Having suffered something of a setback in my political fortunes, I confess that I was drinking more than usual

Meanwhile, Rita and Noah had been at cross-purposes. Noah was convinced that Rita had stood him up because he was black rather than because she had preferred to see Danny Kaye. She said she believed that he was only interested in her as a friend, he had made no attempt to put his arm around her or kiss her when they went to the cinema. Noah's gentlemanly explanation, that he preferred to develop a relationship gradually, caused Rita some puzzlement. Never a lady, she was surprised to be treated like one. Noah invited her to come and hear him play. She agreed.

Thus, on a fateful night for us all, I was surprised to see Rita arrive with Noah as I chatted to Helen at the Flamingo. Noah kindly asked if I had any objections. Given that I was holding Helen's hand at the time, I could hardly say that I did. Helen was particularly happy, telling me that Azzopardi would no longer be a problem. She had told him the relationship was over, and he appeared to have taken the news well. Such generosity did not seem to be in character, but I thought it wiser to say nothing.

Having suffered something of a setback in my political fortunes, I confess that I was drinking more than usual that night. Helen was full of tender concern for my disappointment, while Rita was her usual cynical and unsympathetic self. Sitting rather dizzily between Helen and Rita, who appeared to have forged some kind of womanly

---

24 At the risk of wearying the reader, who may already think that I should be ranked with the dinosaurs which hold a strange attraction for the very young, I should explain that tallymen were door-to-door salesman who provided goods for which they were paid by instalments.

Opposite: *Helen at the Flamingo*

understanding that entirely defeated me, I was surprised to see Azzopardi approaching our table, accompanied by a rather unpleasant-looking man with something of the weasel about his face.

Azzopardi seemed suspiciously friendly, wondering how I was, before seeking an introduction to Rita. In what appeared to be a reflex reaction to a new woman, he flirted mildly with her, asking if she was unaccompanied. She said that she was with someone, indicating Noah. Azzopardi said that a woman as attractive as Rita should not waste her time on 'niggers'. Rita replied levelly that she would like to throw her drink in his face, but it would take more than one gin and tonic to get him clean. At this, the henchman moved forward threateningly, but Azzopardi waved him back, claiming that he had no hard feelings. I warned Rita that she should be careful, revealing that he was the man who had made an entirely unprovoked assault upon my person, using a teapot as an offensive weapon. Rita, unfeelingly, said that he could not be all bad.

The shock of seeing Azzopardi again drove me to the bar for some alcoholic reinforcement. While I was convinced that I was absolutely sober, Helen strongly disagreed, and insisted that we left. As I felt the chill of the night air I staggered somewhat, and then, with Helen supporting me, made towards her car. The sound

A tense moment captured by a strolling photographer. Phil Azzopardi makes his presence felt shortly before his attempt to kill me

of running feet made me turn, to see Azzopardi
waving his henchman on. He had an open razor in
his hand. Urging Helen to call the police I took to
my heels, pursued by the steely-eyed men of
violence. Unfortunately, I ran into a blind alley where
I stood, cornered. Under normal circumstances I
would naturally have taken on both of them, razors
or no, and doubtless given an excellent account of
myself, but my state of inebriation had slowed my
reflexes. As I stood, sobbing quietly and awaiting
my fate, I saw Noah running towards me, clutching
a microphone stand. Events became confused. There
were police whistles and pounding feet. I saw a
razor approaching my cheek, and closed my eyes.
Noah brought the microphone stand down on
Azzopardi's head, with a satisfying thwack. As
Azzopardi fell, his henchman melting into the night,
the police arrived, pinioning Noah. When I tried to
explain that he was bravely defending the person
of a JP and councillor, a policeman cut me short,
saying that I too was under arrest.

*I try to ignore
Azzopardi*

We were taken to West End Central police station
in Vine Street, tucked away behind Piccadilly Circus,
but not tucked away enough in my view. Despite my
protestations, my fingerprints were taken and I was subjected to an entirely
inappropriate interrogation by an unpleasant young man with a small moustache and
a Hitlerian manner. I informed him that my reasons for being in Soho were none of
his affair, rejecting his leering insinuations and resenting particularly his insistence
on calling me 'chummy'. I repeated my story several times for his benefit – that I
had been set upon in an entirely unprovoked assault by Phil Azzopardi and his gang
of seven thugs; that I had been bravely fighting them off, causing considerable physical
damage, until Azzopardi himself had closed in to deliver the *coup de grâce*, at which
point my friend Noah had bravely rescued me.

Ultimately, after a telephone call to my mother of which I was to be reminded
frequently over her remaining years, they were satisfied with my identity and released
me with a caution. Noah, however, was not so fortunate, his black face telling against
him. He was charged with causing Azzopardi grievous bodily harm, and granted
bail at a court hearing the next day, despite strong opposition from the police. My
mother, Helen and I all tried to reassure him about the fairness of British justice,
reminding him that Azzopardi would crack under interrogation as soon as he was
conscious. Unfortunately, he remained stubbornly unconscious, and was reported
to be in a serious condition. Despite Azzopardi's inability to provide a statement,
Noah was due to appear in court where, we anticipated, he would be remanded on
bail for a further hearing.

My mother, despite suffering from a broken ankle, was still keen to accompany us,

Courtroom drama as Noah's bail application is heard

although it was manifestly impossible. She declared that if she was fit she could sort the matter out in no time. We looked at her, amazed. Yes, she said, she would tell the court that Noah and I had been in the house with her on the night in question. As kindly as I could I pointed out that this would be perjury. "Only if they don't believe me," she said.

I had naturally mobilized the resources of my firm to obtain the best possible legal advice for Noah, recruiting one of the brightest younger barristers, Simon Gould, to represent him. I had put some rather juicy cases his way, and felt no compunction in reminding him of this; I would remind him again when he submitted his account.

So it was with some optimism that Noah, Helen and I set out for the court, where we were surprised to find Rita and Lou, Rita declaring that they had come to offer Noah moral support, Lou saying that he would be happy to provide a character reference. Rita was downcast to learn that it would be at least an hour before Noah's case was heard; they were busy in the salon. Noah urged her to go back to work, saying that he appreciated her concern. Rita promised him that they would go out to celebrate that night, then kissed him full on the lips, which caused a certain amount of sensation in the corridor.

Opposite: Noah in the dock

Lou had brought his case of tallyman goods and, to while away the time, attempted to interest Helen in a pair of stockings. As he was waxing lyrical about his rather

I try to save Lou from a night in the cells for contempt of court

inferior stock, I noticed a policeman taking an interest and nudged him. Lou, assuming an unconvincing expression of innocence, closed the lid of his case, catching Helen's hand inside as he did so. Wincing, she removed it as Simon Gould joined us, looking concerned. The hearing had been moved unexpectedly from Court One to Court Three; he felt that the police and the prosecution might be up to something. Although I guessed the answer, I asked Simon who was the Chief Magistrate in Court Three. 'Bray', was the response. My face fell. He was a notorious right winger, who was probably disappointed that Mosley had not become dictator of Britain.

It was with a heavy heart that I joined Helen and Lou at the back of the court, while Noah stood in the dock. Simon made an eloquent case for Noah's bail to be renewed. Bray asked the prosecution to speak. The prosecutor, Howson, said that the police still opposed bail, and had been disappointed when their first application was refused. Bray said that he concurred, since it was not his practice to grant bail to negroes, an utterly shameful statement typical of the man. Simon interjected that Noah had proved his trustworthiness by appearing in court. Howson pointed out that the police investigation was proceeding, and there was no guarantee that Noah would appear when the investigation was complete. It was easy for defendants such as him to disappear back to their place of origin, thus wasting police time. Bray again agreed and, with a quick glance at his fellow magistrates, remanded Noah in custody. Simon made a further attempt to change his mind, but Bray interrupted him, pointing out that Noah had no home of his own, no steady job, and was a jazz musician, a phrase he invested with particular disdain. Simon courageously suggested to Bray that he might be discriminating against Noah on the basis of his colour, but Bray claimed he was not prejudiced, rather spoiling his point by suggesting that Noah could be secreting a "one-way ticket back to Bongo-Bongo Land in his pocket".

Lou suddenly sprang to his feet, shouting at Bray that this was blatant discrimination and a travesty of justice. Bray wondered if he was volunteering to join Noah in the cells. I urged Lou to sit down, since Bray was bound to lock him up. Lou whispered that he had nothing to lose, since he and Margaret were going to spend the weekend with Veronica. In any case, he could not stand by and watch a mate being victimized because of his colour.

Bray instructed a policeman to take Lou into custody, while I tugged at his jacket, fearful of how Margaret would react when she discovered that I had allowed her husband to be imprisoned. Then I had an inspiration; I told Lou that if he was arrested, the contents of his case would be investigated. Lou subsided.

My immediate task was to rescue Noah. The law provides for a judge to overrule a decision of the magistrates, and I urged Simon to seek an immediate hearing. Fortunately a judge was on the premises, so we did not have to go to another court. Then I telephoned Rita to give her the bad news. Calling me a pillock, she slammed down the telephone, reassuring Margaret that it was only me, and not a customer. Fuming, she rampaged around the salon until the phone rang again. This time it was Squadron Leader Cunningham, asking her out. Rita's mood magically changed.

Simon said he had obtained five minutes with the judge, and I asked if I could accompany him. Simon said I could, if I agreed to leave the talking to him. I could not decide whether five minutes with Judge Henshaw would be fruitful or not. He had a reputation for allowing magistrates' decisions to stand unless there was some compelling reason to change them, and Noah's case was not the strongest.

Simon argued that the decision to withhold bail had been made purely on the basis of Noah's colour; a white defendant would have been treated differently. Henshaw said that the issue of colour could not be ignored, and the fact that Noah came from Jamaica was also a consideration. Unable to keep silent, I asked whether there was one law for them and one for us. Peering at me over his glasses, Henshaw said that when the full facts were known, Noah would be judged fairly, but it was important that Noah was in court to be judged, rather than on his way back home. Gathering his papers, Henshaw was about to dismiss us when I decided that I had to speak and asked for a further minute of his time. Henshaw said acidly that he was always willing to further his education, sitting back behind his desk and fixing me with a fierce glare.

I began by asking him if he had served in the First World War, a question to which I already knew the answer. Henshaw said that he had. With a distinguished record? Yes, but he did not see the relevance. How would he feel, I asked, if one of his comrades had been imprisoned for saving his life? Henshaw said that doubtless he would not

We went through everything together, the mud, the bullets ... We didn't think about colour then, we battled on, side by side, fighting for freedom

have been too pleased. I pointed out that Noah had done me that service, carrying on when Henshaw tried to interrupt.

"The other night he saved my life," I said, "and not for the first time. But then we both helped each other out of difficult situations during the war. That's when I met Mr Hawksley. We went through everything together, sir, the mud, the bullets ... We didn't think about colour then. We battled on, side by side, fighting for freedom. Just like you and your comrades, sir."

I wiped away a tear. Henshaw was also moved, and reflected for a moment. Then he asked Simon why he had not been made aware of these circumstances. Simon, quite justifiably, said he had not known about them. Henshaw, reaching for the telephone, said that he would have Noah released immediately. Simon gestured to me, and we left the room before the judge could change his mind. He grinned at me in the corridor, saying that he thought I had served as a clerk in the war. "Okay," I said, "we were filing for freedom. Someone had to do it."

My mother had arranged a special West Indian tea in Noah's honour – well, a tin of pineapple chunks – but Noah was disconsolate, talking of pawning his trumpet and paying his passage home. I pointed out that I would be £50 down if he absconded. Noah said that naturally he would wait until all this was over, then went to his room, returning with pictures of his family to show us. His daughter, Ruthie, was sixteen, and he had been thinking of bringing her over, since she had ambitions to be a nurse. My mother asked, in her direct way, why he was sniffing around Rita if he had a family already. Noah replied that his wife had left him during the war. My mother said it was funny how much he and I had in common, and chuckled. I was again reassuring him that things would return to normal, when there was a knock at the door. I opened it to find a flustered Helen. Azzopardi had gone into a coma.

Either I refused to give incriminating evidence against him, or he would have me cut to ribbons

Things looked bleak, but there was no point in waiting for fate to play its evil hand. What we needed was a witness, or at least the name of Azzopardi's henchman. I told Noah to telephone anyone that he knew who might be able to help. I visited the police in Stoke Newington, who knew my status and treated me accordingly, but Soho was rather off their beat and they had nothing to offer. It was Helen who found the name, having phoned Azzopardi's former wife in Malta. The man was called Marco, he was Azzopardi's cousin, and ran a second-hand car dealership under the arches near St Pancras. We were discussing our next move when I received a worrying telephone call from the Charing Cross Hospital; Azzopardi had become delirious, and was calling my name. The doctor suggested that I should get there immediately.

Azzopardi was in a private room. I knocked on the door, received no reply, turned the knob and went in, to find Azzopardi sitting up in bed playing cards with a large, swarthy individual. I stepped backwards, but Azzopardi called me in, dismissing his bodyguard with a few terse words of what I assumed to be Maltese. He had a proposal to put to me: if I forgot the attack, and forgot that I had seen a razor, then he would forget about Helen. At first the idea seemed appealing, since it removed the threat to me, but it still left Noah facing the music. I refused, pointing out that if it came to his

Opposite: *Lou looking almost intelligent*

•105•

The two Mrs Moons and me

word against mine, a court would doubtless prefer that of an upright British citizen to that of the proprietor of a 'Model Agency' and Soho landlord. I said that I could see no deal. Azzopardi hoped that I was not fond of singing, because I did not have a natural falsetto, and a razor could achieve more than a teapot could. He saw a deal very clearly – either I refused to give incriminating evidence against him, or he would have me cut to ribbons. I told him I would think about it, and left with his laughter ringing in my ears.

I was discussing the matter with Helen after an unusually intimate moment at the maisonette, my mother having gone to have her plaster changed, when Stanley interrupted us, causing us to cut our discussion short, and Helen to mislay a stocking. As she retired modestly, I continued the discussion with Stanley. Azzopardi's deal, I felt, could not be relied on. I could pretend to lose my memory in the witness box, and still wake up one morning to find my wedding tackle in the next room. Helen, who had rejoined us, winced at this. But I had formed a plan, although its success depended on help from Stanley, about whom I had no worries, and from Lou, which was quite another matter.

I broached it to Lou over a cup of tea in Joe Lyons. Unfortunately Margaret was present, but when I explained that no danger was involved, and the plan depended for its success on the intelligence and cunning for which he was well known, Lou was won over.

That was why the afternoon found Lou admiring Marco's used cars. Marco, sensing a mug on the premises, gave Lou all his attention. Lou asked if he was interested in a part-exchange, a pre-war Bugatti for the heap of rust they were standing beside. Marco did his best to appear uninterested, asking Lou if he lived locally. Lou said he came from Hackney, at which Marco gave an exclamation of delight – he happened to be passing there that very night. Lou gave him the address, then nearly spoiled the plan by turning and raising his thumbs towards the corner where I was lurking with my hat over my eyes and my collar turned up. Part one of the plan was achieved; I immediately went to put the second part into operation.

Stanley interrupted us, causing us to cut our discussion short, and Helen to mislay a stocking

When Marco arrived, Lou and Stanley were waiting outside the garage that held the supposed Bugatti, Lou nervous, Stan armed with a billiard cue secreted up his sleeve in case of trouble. They opened the garage doors, and Marco peered inside, turning with an expression of anger on his face. The car was not a rare Bugatti but a common or garden Wolseley Twelve, As he sought an explanation I stepped from the shadows, pretending a calmness which I did not feel, and greeted him. Marco, alarmed, tried to retreat, but found Stanley behind him, the billiard cue now on full display. Like so many of his kind when the odds are against them, Marco immediately began to whine, claiming that the assault had nothing to do with him, that it had all been at Phil's instigation. It had been Phil with the razor, not him. He had been an unwilling participant, Phil was a known gangster, no one had been more surprised than Marco at the turn events had taken, Phil had been consumed by jealousy, Marco had tried to stop him, it was a cowardly attack and if Noah had not intervened, then I would probably be dead. He paused for breath, looking at me with pleading in his eyes. I raised a hand to stop him, while Stanley slid his weapon back into his sleeve. Then I called on my policeman friend who had been hiding in the car with a notebook. I was sure that, if he had missed anything, Marco would be pleased to repeat it.

CHAPTER SIX

THE REVOLVING DOOR OF FATE

I N THE JUNGLE THAT IS POLITICS, it is not necessarily the lion who triumphs over the three-toed sloth, to coin a phrase.[25] Not, of course, that I see myself as a sloth, more a gazelle. Be that as it may, the first six months of 1953 saw me raised to the heights, dashed to the ground, dashed even further to the ground, then raised again. Truly, fate is a revolving door, precipitating one sometimes into the lobby of the five-star hotel, sometimes into the gutter.

I have already noted that an unruly left-wing element was seeking to raise a clamour in Hackney. I therefore determined to apply to become a parliamentary candidate, first approaching my union, the Clerical Workers, which sponsored a number of MPs. They in turn put my name forward to the party, with the result that I was summoned to a meeting in Transport House, and placed on the 'A' list of candidates. Sid Jupp, our jovial general secretary, was only too happy to oblige me, since I had ensured that the union received legal advice from the firm under very generous terms. It was also helpful that I had mistakenly entered the wrong hotel room at Blackpool, to find Sid

Opposite: *An early champagne socialist*

25. This is an original coinage, and is available to the compilers of anthologies without any question of copyright, although a copy of the anthology would be welcome.

Stanley was looking forward to his demob

and his secretary exploring another meaning of the word congress.

It was with a certain sense of triumph that I announced my good news at the first possible opportunity, a meeting of the housing committee. Although our personal relations were at a low ebb, I nonetheless received genuine congratulations from Avis, who declared that the Parliamentary Party needed new blood. She urged me to inform the selection committee that militancy did not mean Communism, and that complacency was not good Socialism. I said that I appreciated her advice, particularly since we were no longer a couple, and suggested that we might still be friends. Avis said that she had been seeking more than friendship. I told her, with tears in my eyes and a lump in my throat, that she deserved more than I could offer her. Brushing this aside, although obviously touched, Avis urged me to assert myself. I told her that I stood for the working man, for blokes who had struggled against the odds all their lives.

"That's right!" she exclaimed. "Men who go out to work at some ungodly hour, and come home after dark, dog-tired, and have to scrub themselves down in the kitchen sink. Men who work in coal-mines and shipyards and steel mills!" I had to tell her that the by-election was in Surrey.

My mother at first thought that Carshalton Beeches was a seaside constituency, but when I told her it was near Croydon, and there was a large Conservative majority, she thought that she might wait to buy a new hat to celebrate my achievement.

I travelled by train to the meeting of the selection committee, deliberately arriving early so that I could sniff the air and assess the lie of the land. Carshalton Beeches was certainly a world away from Hackney. The streets were quiet, the houses neat, the trees manicured, the people well-spoken. There was a tennis club. When I stopped for tea, it was in the Windsor Tea Rooms, where the waitresses wore black with starched white aprons and starched caps. I felt like a resistance fighter on a mission behind enemy lines.

Jane Goodhew, the local agent, was very welcoming, and seemed willing to be pumped for information. The committee was of seven people, she said, two of whom I had already met at Transport House, and who would be on my side. I asked what kind of candidate they were seeking. Jane ducked the question, advising me to be myself. But she did volunteer the useful information that they leaned towards the progressive wing of the party, were sceptical of union power, supported rearmament, and had recently taken a keen interest in the issue of immigration, believing it to be a moral and emotional issue on which the party should take a lead. I felt immediately relieved; having Noah in my spare room could be crucial to my success.

I told her, with tears in my eyes and a lump in my throat, that she deserved more than I could offer her

As is my normal practice, I spoke frankly and fearlessly to the committee, trying to work out the answers which were required of me, then offering them. Sometimes my principles had to take a back seat, but such is politics. The committee seemed certainly to be on my side, but there was a major stumbling block – they wanted to meet my family. I assured them that my family would be on parade should they choose me as the candidate, and that there were no skeletons in my cupboard. I was a devoted father, I supported my old mum, and I believed in a harmonious family as the basis of society. In that case, said the chairman, I was welcome aboard!

That night Stanley was holding a party to celebrate his demob from the RAF and his return to civilian life. Thanks to my selection meeting I was late, and distractedly squeezed past Dilys on my way to the kitchen in search of beer. The family was gathered around the table, but as ever with the Moons, harmony was notable by its absence. Rita had been flirting with Noah before he left for the Flamingo, almost colliding in the doorway with Squadron Leader Cunningham who was arriving. Margaret strongly disapproved, and was telling her mother so. Calling for a bit of hush, I told them that they were looking at a new Labour Party candidate, and that I had promised a full family turnout at my first public meeting to show the voters that Harvey Moon was a true family man. Rita immediately accused me of hypocrisy. Margaret said that she would be present, and so would Lou. She and Rita began

A disappointing night in Carshalton Beeches

sniping at one another, then Stanley got involved. My mother brought the discussion to a close by slamming a saucepan against the draining board, producing immediate silence. I had been a good husband and a good father, she said, never asking the family for anything. Now I had, and everyone would be on parade at the meeting, or they could reckon with her.

So the following Tuesday in the hall of the Women's Institute, I was able to address the voters of Carshalton Beeches (or as many as had bothered to attend) with a crescent of Moons on the platform behind me.

"I believe that this country is like a family," I declared, again with moisture in my eyes and a lump in my throat, for sincerity has always come easily to me, particularly on public occasions. "Of course there's disagreement, of course there's discord. But there's a common thread of pride and decency, a desire to make things better than they are, and better for the families of the future!" Even I was surprised at the level of applause.

From then on it was a constant round of knocking on inhospitable doors, addressing empty streets from a loudspeaker van, attempting to shake hands with the uninterested, and to press leaflets on those in a hurry. Although I was the victor in my dreams, I knew that the Conservative majority was impregnable. Helen was a tower of strength as I made my way, exhausted to the Flamingo club each night, occupying what was now my regular bar stool while Noah played. Her loyalty and encouragement were such that I almost believed in the possibility of a miracle. Coincidentally, I developed quite a taste for jazz in that period, although I could never tell the difference between be-bop and swing. I now lean towards the delightful musicality of James Last and his Orchestra, as I would have proved had the late Roy Plomley invited me to appear on Desert Island Discs. For some reason, the call never came.

At last it was the night of the count, and my dreams were finally put to rest. The Tory, magnanimous in victory, shook my hand and congratulated me on my performance. Since I had docked his majority by eight thousand, I was not certain that his congratulations were genuine, but he assured me that they were, and that I had fought an excellent campaign. Advising me to stay with the moderates, he promised that he would buy me a brown ale in the Commons bar when I found a more winnable seat. Helen, who had loyally come to support me, produced a bottle of champagne, which amused the good Brigadier greatly; I was pleased to inform him that Socialists, too, could enjoy the finer things of life.

Sincerity has always come easily to me, especially on public occasions

So, licking my wounds, I returned to the mundane round of Council affairs in Hackney. After my exploits in Carshalton Beeches, I found it hard to summon up my old enthusiasm for the weary round of committees and sub-committees, the points of order and endless bickering. Looking around at my colleagues on the housing committee, I found their self-righteousness and limited horizons particularly wearisome. I was now a man who had fought the good fight in an enemy stronghold, a man who had carried the Red Flag into hostile territory. Surely life should hold more than the left-wing firebrand Randall making an interminable speech about the number of council houses we had promised

Moon, magnanimous in defeat

but failed to build? Perhaps rudely, I interrupted him, pointing out that we were attempting a mixture of public and private enterprise, and that houses would be allocated on a strict rota basis, except in case of special need. Here I declared an interest. Given my mother's broken ankle, and the difficulties she faced coping with the stairs to the maisonette, I had promised her that I would use my influence to obtain a ground floor flat. I told the committee that my mother was a case of special need, and that we would be submitting an application for rehousing. Randall immediately said that there could be no special favours, and no queue-jumping.

I was about to bring the Moon eloquence into play, when Avis joined the debate, saying that while my mother might qualify, she wondered whether I did. As a well-paid white-collar worker, I was surely in a position to look for rented accommodation? Randall naturally concurred, and I could sense that the mood of the meeting was against me. I decided to fight another day, and went to see Helen for consolation.

I had promised to obtain a television set for my mother to watch the Coronation

Call it love, call it preoccupation, call it disillusionment, call it what you will, but I confess that my mind was not entirely on Council matters. I was fully aware that my re-selection meeting for Down's Ward was imminent, but as a local celebrity and sitting member I felt that re-selection would be a formality, particularly since my opponent was the insignificant figure of Gordon Hopkins, whose militant brand of politics was not, in my view, appealing to the good people of Down's Ward.

The weather on the night of the meeting was appalling, with rain lashing the streets, driven by a cold east wind. Not surprisingly, there were few people in the committee room when I arrived, but suddenly a group of men arrived, ushered in by Hopkins. Their faces were new to me and I felt a premonition. I asked Hopkins who they were. He said that he had been running a recruitment drive, and had organized a rota of people with cars to make sure of a good attendance. I approached Avis who was chairing the meeting, suggesting that it should be postponed to a more clement night, with the unspoken thought that I could then arrange for my own supporters to be present. Somewhat snappily, she said that there was a quorum, and called the meeting to order. As sitting candidate, I spoke first, referring to my unbroken record of service and unceasing devotion to the ward and the party. Hopkins then launched into a fierce tirade, not naming me but implying that I was complacent, lazy, self-seeking and uninterested in Hackney. They were lies of course, damnable lies, but they drew considerable applause.

The first vote was a tie, and Avis invited another. This, too, was a tie and so, using her casting vote, she declared for Hopkins. I was outraged. How could this woman, to whom I had given so much of myself, betray me? As I attempted to pursue the matter, Hopkins came up and asked if she was ready to go. They left arm in arm, partners in a plot of such deviousness and ingratitude that even now it beggars belief, a mousy Eve and her pint-sized snake in the grass who had not only planned my assassination, but had also brought tragedy to the people of Hackney. *Et tu*, Avis!

These devastating events were still preying on my mind as Coronation Day dawned, a momentous event in the life of the nation, the dawn of a new Elizabethan age. Rather more republican then than I am now, I was less concerned with the royal foldero than

with my own prospects – the dawn of a new Moon age would have suited me better. *Rita found Lou a*
But there was enough on my domestic plate to keep my mind from grander designs. *far from ideal*
I had promised to obtain a television set for my mother to watch the Coronation, but *son-in-law*
the matter had slipped my mind in the press of political events and, when I got round
to it, there were no sets to be had. Even Noah, the mildest of men, joined in the entirely
unjustified criticism of my failure. I had, after all, made arrangements for us to join
the residents and staff of a nearby old people's home, but my mother took this as an
attempt to incarcerate her by underhand means, and was having none of it. In actual
fact, concern about my mother's increasing age, and the diminishing pleasures of
using my office as a place to be with Helen, had led my mind to wander. Would my
mother not be happier with other old people, leaving me with more freedom at home?
I immediately dismissed the thought as unworthy, despite the very reasonable terms
that the matron of the home had offered.

Hence in Moon household one, as it might be thought of, the atmosphere was
definitely frosty, as it was in Moon household two, where Rita had suffered an abrupt
awakening at an early hour. Unable to sleep, Lou had gone to the kitchen to make
himself a mug of Bournvita and, while there, had turned on the wireless. What he
heard made him rush up the stairs as quickly as his lung allowed, waking first Margaret
and then her mother. He had momentous news – Mount Everest had been conquered
by an Englishwoman called Hilary and her sheep Tensing! Rita, her brain befogged
by the hour and the previous night's intake of gin, considered this preposterous notion
quite seriously. Granted, she said, an Englishwoman might have climbed the mountain,
but not with a sheep. Maggie suggested that it might have been a yak. Lou believed
this to be the obvious solution.

The household was still in ferment when my mother telephoned to speak to Rita but found Lou on the end of the line. Excitedly he put forward his news. My mother said that she did not know what a yak was. Lou explained that it was an exotic long-haired cow. My mother said that, talking of exotic long-haired cows, was Rita there? Unfortunately, Lou had handed the receiver to Rita, who reacted strongly to the insult. My mother, most unusually, launched into a lengthy apology for their present and past misunderstandings. Rita interrupted, asking what it was that my mother wanted. She wanted to watch Rita's newly-installed television.

My former wife yielded with an ill grace, comforting herself with the thought that Noah would be coming with us. But her temper was not improved when Stanley came downstairs, wearing a suit and tie and announcing that he was off to see the Coronation itself from a balcony in Lower Regent Street rather than staying to watch it on television. He thought that he might not be able to return for the neighbourhood Coronation party. As Rita tried to argue with him, and Margaret accused him of feeling ashamed of his family, Stanley sidled away.

I, too, had been entertaining doubts about Stanley, wondering whether he was in danger of becoming a class-climber. His new-found ambitions had been fanned into life during a brief period when he worked as a street photographer with an unsavoury young man called Lenny. While Stanley dreamed of becoming Cecil Beaton, Lenny dreamed of being rich. He roamed far and wide in search of custom, specializing in *Rita takes French* tourist venues on Bank Holiday weekends. One such had found the two young men *leave with Tim* at Syon Park, a stately home and garden near London, where Lenny took the pictures

while Stanley took the money and details of the customers so that prints could be forwarded. At first all went well, but soon Stanley became aware that Lenny was using two cameras. If a customer said he was from London, one camera was used, but if he came from further afield, then the other was called into play. Stanley noticed that the second camera appeared to contain an unlimited amount of film, and asked Lenny about it. Lenny refused to give a straight answer, and the conversation was interrupted when an elderly couple and an attractive girl asked if their picture could be taken. When the girl said that they were from Maidenhead, Lenny raised the second camera, while Stanley held the first. As the girl was walking away, Stanley offered to change the film in Lenny's camera. Lenny refused to give it to him, but Stanley grabbed it and opened the back. As he had suspected, the camera was empty – there was no film. Giving Lenny a hefty shove in the chest, Stanley tossed the empty camera into a bush and made off with the day's takings and the other camera, pursued by Lenny's plaintive cries.

My mother said that, talking of long-haired exotic cows, was Rita there?

After some minutes' searching, he caught up with the girl and her relations, claiming that there had been a technical problem, and refunding their ten shillings. He and the girl looked at one another for a moment, then Stanley turned away. He was strongly attracted, but she was obviously out of his class. The older man, who turned out to be an uncle, called him back. He was sure that Esme would like some company of her own age, and Stanley seemed such an honest young man ... would he care to join them for tea?

Tea, followed by a ride on the steam train, led to an exchange of confidences, of names and addresses and telephone numbers, then to cinema visits. Suddenly Aircraftsman Stanley Moon, trainee draughtsman and part-time street photographer, was moving in a world he had never before experienced. Esme's mother was a languid society hostess, her father was an architect successful enough to have a large West End office. Whatever reservations they may have had about my rough diamond son they did not voice them, since Esme was so obviously keen on Stanley, and Stanley was so obviously devoted to her. It was Esme who invited Stanley to watch the Coronation from the office balcony, and her mother who suggested that he bring a camera so that he could take pictures of her guests. Esme could have Stanley's company, her mother could have a photographer who would not charge for his services.

Margaret was still griping about Stanley as Rita turned on the television, to be greeted with a hailstorm, behind which something that may have been Buckingham Palace was moving to and fro. Lou, meditating on whether Battenberg cake had been named after the Duke of Edinburgh, or vice versa, claimed that he knew about televisions, and suggested that the problem might lie in the horizontal hold. Rita said she was not familiar with the expression. Margaret said she was surprised, given Rita's wartime experiences, and suggested that the aerial might need adjustment. Rita told Lou to go up to the roof and adjust it, waving aside his fears that he might get indigo. Margaret said he could reach it from the box room window. Sighing, Lou went to do as he was told, while Rita wondered whether it was legally possible to divorce a son-in-law.

Coronation Day, a momentous event for the nation and me

"I'm leaning out the window, and I've got it firmly in my hand," Lou shouted down to the two women. "Wiggle it about," Margaret responded. The picture worsened. Lou moved the aerial in the other direction, magically improving the picture. It was certainly Buckingham Palace. "Hold it like that," Margaret shouted, but even as she spoke she saw a familiar shape fall past the window, landing with a crash in the flowerbed. Lou had lost his balance.

Meanwhile, Stanley was trying to cope with a large number of potentially hostile people. Since he was nervous, he had drunk rather more sherry than was good for him, the elegant morsels of food served by a maid insufficient to mop up the effects of the alcohol. He would have been happier with beer, but none was on offer. Esme's mother, Mrs Sibley, smiled vaguely at him as she circulated among her guests, never quite staying long enough to hear the end of a story. Esme herself was enjoying Stanley's company, and hoping that she could bring a secret plan to fruition.

The young couple were approached by Charles Critchley, a friend of the Sibleys, and Esme's godfather. He kissed her on the cheek, telling her that she was developing fast. Esme blushed, then introduced the two men. Critchley looked Stanley up and down, asking if his family were from Maidenhead, since he had not seen Stan at the tennis club. Stanley said that he and Esme had met at Syon Park. Critchley wanted to know if he was connected to the Percys: Stanley said that it sounded painful. Ignoring this, Critchley explained that it was the Percys' southern seat, and Esme came to the rescue with the information that Percy was the family name of the Duke of Northumberland.

Stanley, who had taken an instant dislike to Critchley, offered that his friend Roy was from Northumberland, and that his father was involved in coal-mining. Critchley suggested that nationalization must have been something of a setback, to which Stanley replied that Roy's father was a shop steward, and had welcomed the pits being taken into public ownership. Critchley grunted, then walked off to talk to Esme's father. Esme herself did not appear happy, and Stanley attempted to mollify her by explaining that he had been joking. Since Critchley was a snob, surely she could sympathize? Esme told him that Critchley was a snob who published an architectural magazine which might have an opening for a photographer, then ran off to cry in the lavatory, leaving young Stanley aghast. Had he destroyed his chance of launching on his ideal career? Why hadn't Esme told him? Stanley went to find Esme and mend his fences.

Meanwhile, my mother, Noah and I had arrived at Rita's. I had brought a bottle of Scotch to add to the gaiety, while my mother had brought a tin of Coronation shortbread, although she said she would like the tin back as a souvenir. My mother, plonking herself down in the middle chair so as to obtain the best view, asked Rita why the television was showing only snow. Had they obtained pictures of Mount Everest already? Rita explained that it had only worked when Lou had gone upstairs to adjust the aerial, but that unfortunately he had fallen out of the window. I was immediately concerned, particularly when Rita said that he had gone to the hospital with Margaret, but she said that he was conscious, or rather as conscious as he ever was. When I asked what the matter was, she suggested that he had probably been dropped on his head at birth. I was scandalised at this typical lack of feeling, and told her so. My mother was more concerned with the lack of a picture, but Noah was already on his knees, fiddling with the television. He soon found the problem – a loose valve. Had Rita been banging it, he wondered? My mother said that she had been banging it since 1939.

I had brought a bottle of Scotch to add to the gaiety, while my mother had brought a tin of Coronation shortbread

With the valve correctly in its socket, a picture formed, and there were the crowds outside Westminster Abbey in living black and white. Rita, thrilled, went to embrace Noah, who recoiled; the tension was evident. My mother announced that she was going to spend a penny, while I said that I would put the kettle on. We exited speedily, leaving them to their own devices, although it was easy for me to hear every word. In any case, I knew what the problem was, since Noah and I had discussed it into the night. The problem was Rita, or rather Rita's inability to be content with one man at a time.

Noah was justifiably confused by the signals he had been receiving. She had come to hear him play, had come to the court, had made him feel that he was important to her. When they had tried to gain admission to a dance at the Conservative Club and had been denied on account of Noah's colour, she had made an eloquent case against the despicable attitude they encountered. Noah, a serious man with honourable intentions, felt quite rightly that a woman who could defend him so strongly was committed to him and to some kind of exclusive relationship. He did not know at the time that she had simultaneously been seeing Squadron Leader Cunningham, and giving him the same impression of commitment.

Matters came to a head when Cunningham telephoned the salon and invited Rita to lunch. She was surprised when Cunningham arrived at eleven o'clock in the morning, asking whether she was ready to leave. He said that they were having lunch in Deauville. Rita thought that lunch in France was a ridiculous idea, and said that for some reason she had forgotten to bring her passport to work. Cunningham declared that for him, frontiers did not exist! As she left, Rita instructed Margaret to tell anyone who telephoned that she was going "up France" for lunch. And if no one telephoned, Margaret should start ringing round to tell them. When Margaret told Lou where Rita had gone, explaining that Deauville was in France, Lou looked at her pityingly. Of course he knew that; it was famous. Deauville was where kippers came from. This was a complicated theory, even for Lou, and took some untangling. Ultimately, it transpired that Lou had been thinking of Dover sole, so perhaps Rita was correct in her assumption that he had been dropped on his head at birth.

Although I was sitting in a house in Tottenham, it felt as if I was there in Westminster Abbey

Over lunch, accompanied by several bottles of wine, Cunningham told Rita that he had been asked to leave the RAF, due to a misunderstanding over some bouncing cheques. He had been offered a job with Massey-Ferguson in Kenya; would she go with him as his wife? Rita was stunned. Their occasional meetings had involved fun and flirtation – she had even suspected a wife in the background, and nothing had made her think that a proposal was on the cards. She was still mulling it over when they reached the aerodrome and discovered that the aeroplane needed a spare part. Then she was suspicious. Was this a pilot's equivalent of running out of petrol? Was this talk of marriage merely an excuse to get her into bed? What did those rattling crates contain which were being hoisted on board? She had drunk too much wine and too much brandy to think straight. The difficult questions could wait until the morning, and she had no intention of travelling home by sea. So she accepted Tim's suggestion that they should stay in a hotel, although she was not too drunk to forget that she should telephone Margaret. In those days, cross-Channel calls had to be booked through an operator. It was therefore unfortunate that, when the connection was made, Rita was in the throes of passion and ignored the ringing telephone.

Margaret, at the other end of the line, was confronted with an operator who could not speak English, and immediately jumped to conclusions. There had been some disaster. Rita was in danger. The plane had crashed! She rushed around to the maisonette to share her news, which did not go down well with Noah. He was more concerned that Rita was in France with Tim than with Margaret's babblings about possible disaster. To calm her, I agreed to telephone the police, advised by Stanley that Elstree would be the most likely airfield to be used for a private trip. Thus it was that when Rita and Cunningham arrived there, and as the crates were being unloaded, they were met by a policeman who, having assured himself of Rita's well-being, took a keen interest in the crates. Rita was past caring, since it had been a bumpy ride, and particularly since Cunningham had disclaimed all knowledge of the conversation in which he had talked of marriage and Kenya, accusing her of inventing the entire exchange.

Noah's disillusionment was profound, and he accused Rita of caring nothing for his feelings. He told her that he was a proud man, and could not cope with her being affectionate one minute, cold the next. In particular, he had been distraught to learn about her jaunt to France. Rita assured him that any relationship with Tim was over. Noah said he was sure that there would be another Tim to tempt her with a fast car or a yacht. Exercising all the charm with which she was equipped, the charm that had snared me years before and to which I was still occasionally susceptible, Rita told Noah that she fancied him. Weakening, Noah said that this was not enough; after all, one could fancy a bag of chips after a night at the pictures, and it meant nothing. Pressing herself against him, Rita said he was at least a fish supper.

My mother, re-entering, interrupted a kiss. "Blimey," she said, "I washed my hands for a good five minutes!"

And so we sat down to watch the Coronation. I am not too proud to confess that I wiped away a tear as the young Princess, so small and slight, and taking on such

God Save The Queen!

*The Squadron
Leader and the
easily led*

vast responsibilities, became our Queen, with all the pomp and circumstance that is so peculiarly and wonderfully British. Although I was sitting in a house in Tottenham, it felt as if I was there in Westminster Abbey. Even Rita, for whom the expression 'hard-boiled' could have been invented, was moved.

The Sibley party was equally enthralled, although Mrs Sibley was not so transported that she forgot to remind Stanley of his photographic duties. Reconciled with Esme, his concern now was to prove himself to Critchley, which is why he made some play with light-meter and focus, offering his subjects a running commentary on his photographic expertise. Having taken the pictures, Stanley made for Critchley, and said he hoped that his earlier comments had not been taken as rude. Critchley replied that miners were the salt of the earth; it was just that he had never met anybody who knew one personally.

That was the great benefit of National Service, Stanley said, it was a great leveller, allowing one to meet all sorts and conditions of men. That was why he had turned down the chance of a commission, rejecting the opportunity of following in his father's footsteps for an opportunity to mingle with the working classes. He was nevertheless proud to have a father with a distinguished war record, who was now a solicitor and a parliamentary candidate. 'A Conservative?' interjected Critchley. 'What else,' my devious son replied. He had to confess that Esme had told him about Critchley's magazine, and since he was keen to make a career in photography ... Critchley said that he might be able to find something suitable. Would Stanley care to telephone his secretary to make an appointment?

Esme had been doing some discreet eavesdropping, and joined Stanley as Critchley walked off. She was pleased that Stan had made a good impression, but slightly miffed that he had revealed things to her godfather of which she was unaware. Perhaps Stanley had been too preoccupied with her blouse buttons to talk about his family? She had no idea that I was a war hero and a stalwart Tory. Stanley said that he liked her parents, and Esme immediately wondered whether she would like his. Why not go and see how the other party was getting on? Stanley told her that it would be very dull, full of stodgy people discussing law and politics. Esme thought she could cope. Increasingly desperate, Stanley said that it was a long journey. Esme said she would borrow her mother's car. Stanley knew when he was beaten.

The Moon family arrived a little late at the party, where my mother immediately busied herself with making sandwiches, while Noah and I explored the bar. A two-piece band, of accordion and double bass, was torturing an innocent piece of music. Rita insisted that Noah join them and, ignoring his protestations, pulled him towards the stage. Searching through the sheet music, he found 'Bye Bye Blackbird' and launched into it, even taking the opportunity to sing. My mother, somewhat raucously, joined in. I had invited Helen to join me, and was greatly relieved to see her arrive, together with two of the regular band from the Flamingo. Then, just as Noah had reached the section of the song that refers to hard luck stories, Margaret and Lou came through the door, Lou's arm in a large plaster cast, with a red, white and blue ribbon pinned to it. Noah winked at him.

Margaret made immediately for the bar and demanded a large brandy. Her husband, she said, had suffered a terrible shock. We gathered round, concerned. I asked Lou what the matter was. Lou said it was his arm. Was it broken? asked my mother. Worse, said Lou gloomily, it was fractured. And that was not the bad news. The doctor had given him a thorough inspection, and had told him that, for a man with his medical history, he was as fit as a flea! He had a good mind to seek a second opinion! We could not contain ourselves; to Lou's surprise and Margaret's anger, hysteria reigned.

And so the party went on, everyone drinking rather too much, children running between the dancers' feet, enjoying an unusually late night, the music improving as the hour grew late. Noah beckoned to Helen, who joined the band for a smoky version of 'Makin' Whoopee', which she sang beautifully. I leaned on the side of the stage looking up at her, feeling suddenly depressed. Everyone had a future, it seemed, except me.

Helen finished her song and joined me, telling me to cheer up because it might never happen. I responded that I was nearly forty-seven, my job was in a rut, my political ambitions were a joke. The only bright spot was us. Rather to my surprise, I

Stanley's friend Roy, an unlikely harbinger of fate

told her that I loved her; I had never said it before. She kissed me, whispering that even if I didn't mean it, she wouldn't stop sleeping with me. Anyway, if I was optimistic, something would turn up. I wondered how she could be so sure. Because, she said, when she was feeling low, I had turned up.

As we danced, my mood now magically improved, someone did turn up, although I had my face buried in Helen's hair at the time, and so missed his entrance. The unlikely harbinger of a brighter future was Roy, Stanley's old RAF chum, who was disappointed that Stan was not there. Margaret told him, with a toss of the head, that the company was not good enough for his lady friend. As the music ended and we joined the family, Roy said that he wanted to speak to me, but our attention was diverted by the arrival of Stanley and Esme. Roy made straight for his friend, followed closely by the family, since none of us had met Esme before.

Rita, assuming her most ladylike tones, introduced herself, as did I. Margaret, in a poor impression of a Pearly Queen, said that she was Stanley's skin and blister, and that we was 'avin' a

right royal time of it and no mistake. Esme recoiled slightly, while clinging to her social smile. Lou told Maggie not to be rude, introduced himself, and told Esme that if she needed anything in the way of lingerie, cosmetics or other feminine accoutrements, she had only to ask. Margaret asked Lou why he was showing her up, Lou replied that manners cost nothing, and she stormed off, Lou in pursuit. "Newlyweds", I said with a shrug, and followed.

Stanley reassured Esme that Margaret's dislike was aimed at him, not her. Roy, never overly diplomatic, asked him why. Because, Stan said, she felt he was ashamed of the family, which was not fair. He had just been uncertain as to whether Esme would like them. Did she like them? Esme had to confess that it was not love at first sight, and was he sure that his father was a prospective Tory candidate? Roy spluttered into his beer at that one.

Perhaps a new career was not out of the question. Orient could do with a good manager

Making a decision, Esme said that the car was outside, the night was still relatively young, and she had no intention of spending her time swilling brown ale and doing the Lambeth Walk. Stanley, frightened that she had been going to leave alone, cheered up, pronounced the evening vulgar, and followed her quickly before she changed her mind.

Poor Roy, left alone, came to find me. He wondered whether I was still interested in politics. I told him that I was no longer sure. In many ways it was a thankless task, trying to help people who invariably thought you were trying to pull a fast one. You had to fight unwinnable seats, and everyone thought you were in it for yourself, no one believed you had a sense of service … I stared moodily into my glass. Perhaps a new career was not out of the question. Orient could do with a good manager.

Roy jerked me from my reverie. "So you wouldn't be interested in a safe Labour seat?" he asked. Putting a finger to my lips, I led him to a quiet corner and asked how a safe Labour seat could be in the gift of a trainee bank clerk? Roy said that his uncle Gideon was secretary of the local party in Burslem, and the sitting member was retiring at the next election to take up caravanning. He had a majority of seven thousand. I said that surely a local candidate would be preferred. Roy told me that he had mentioned me to his uncle, and discovered the good Gideon had held me in high esteem since I played for Orient at Port Vale before the war in the FA Cup. It was not an occasion that I wished to remember, since I had scored two own goals. Apparently it was this unfortunate feat which had commended me, and Roy felt it might be worth my while to visit the Potteries. I had not known that Burslem was in the Potteries, but I thought that my loyal secretary could perhaps undertake some research on my behalf. If Roy could find out what concerned the local party, if I went up to take the temperature, if I polished some of my Carshalton speeches, then surely … Suddenly, the world seemed a brighter place.

Margaret Moon and her old dad, the A-Team!

S O THERE YOU HAVE IT. It is time to lay down the pen and retire to muse among the roses. The floribundas have been particularly fine this year. I shall lean on the arm of my darling daughter, who has been constantly at my side to refresh my memory where it has faltered, and to ensure that the domestic staff do not disturb me. I shall listen to the song of the birds, content with a job well done. By tonight, the house will be empty, the eager young researchers will have departed for a well-earned weekend break before they return on Monday, poised to start afresh on the third volume of these reminiscences. Again the mysterious computers will hum, and flashing fingers record the words of Moon!

In many ways, I am eager to continue, since there is so very much more to tell. I wish to paint for you the panoply of Burslem, immortalized by the great Arnold Bennett, and graced by my own years as its thrusting Member. I wish to tell you tales of the great names of Labour – Bessie Braddock, Bob Mellish, Colonel George Wigg, all sadly no longer with us and, alas, forgotten, except when old Socialists gather for a glass of claret and a Havana cigar to talk about the days when Camelot came to Downing Street in the person of 'King' Harold.

My part in the Profumo affair, my unwitting involvement in the Great Train Robbery, my friendship with the Beatles, all must wait, as must further tales of the family, whose exploits would surely provide the basis for an amusing television series. I may even suggest it! I wonder if Mel Gibson might be persuaded to play the younger me?

Margaret, ever vigilant, informs me that I am maundering, so I shall weary you no longer. Tomorrow is another day, and as I hope you have learned from this brief episode in a full life, every cloud has a silver lining, words which I have often used to comfort those in need. I trust that they may comfort you.

MOON
The Old Rectory
Charlestone-by-Barry
September 1995

Opposite: *My retirement portrait by Gustave Banks, RA*